NETJETTER SUE

Sue Stubbings

To Sharon

Best wishes

from Sue.

2QT Limited (Publishing)

First Edition published 2014 by
2QT Limited (Publishing)
Tatham Fell Lancaster LA2 8RE, United Kingdom

Publisher Disclaimer:
The events in this travel book are described according to the Authors'
recollection; recognition and understanding of the events and individuals
mentioned and are in no way intended to mislead or offend. As such the
Publisher does not hold any responsibility for any inaccuracies or opinions
expressed by the author. Every effort has been made to acknowledge and
gain any permission from organisations and persons mentioned in this
book. Any enquiries should be directed to the author.

Cover Design by Hilary Pitt
Cover Illustrations supplied by shutterstock.com
Photographs © Sue Stubbings

Printed and bound in the UK by Berforts Information Press
The Printer uses FSC and PEFC accredited paper suppliers

A CIP catalogue record for this book is available
from the British Library

ISBN 978-1-910077-31-3

Acknowledgements

First and foremost I would like to thank my wonderful children Ben, Sam and Rachel for their encouragement and the music tapes that comforted me on my journey.

I owe a lot to Gavin Thomas who wielded a vicious cyber red pen while editing my early drafts.

This book has had an extended gestation and my long-suffering proofreaders; Rosy Elliot, Lesley Stevenson (lovers of travel writing), Geoff Clarke and Ben Stubbings (pedants) deserve a special thanks.

Finally I would like to thank the Guardian for choosing me to undertake a journey I would never have dreamed possible.

Contents

The Journey

PROLOGUE

Just before…

Although this journey was undertaken at the beginning of a new century, it took place just before the explosion of the new age of technology. Cyberspace was in its infancy. Although internet cafes were springing up all round the world the computers and connections were often poor and ill-equipped to cope with transmission of photographs. Digital cameras were at an early stage of development and to send photographs each week I had a camera that used floppy discs. The age of universal mobile phones had not yet arrived and the IPhone and IPad were still twinkles in Apple's eye.

The Guardian competition was part of the media's move towards on-line content with the launch of its Travel website. The Netjetter concept was designed to be interactive, with readers actively engaging with the site through email; although the word had not yet been invented, today my reports would have been called blogs.

It also occurred just before the upsurge of older 'grey' backpackers. Round-the-world tickets were available but used mostly for student gap-years. The post-war baby-boomers had not yet reached retirement when they could spend the assets gained from living through an age of almost full employment, rocketing house-prices and generous final salary pensions, which many chose to spend on travel.

Two months after I returned home, an event occurred that changed travel and perhaps the world for ever: the attack on the twin towers on 9-11. Several places I visited have subsequently endured attack – Bali and Mumbai in particular. My passage through multiple airports, large and small, did involve varying degrees of security but far less than after this event. I encountered so much diversity but it manifested itself in standards of living and culture rather than race or religion. I felt no threat to me as a foreign western tourist.

I feel very lucky to have had my adventure at this time in history.

1

The Prize

My second midlife crisis was looming. I knew I was near the edge when all I could bear to read was the job section in the newspaper. In one advert the strange word 'Netjetter' caught my eye.

Are you interested in travelling the world and talking to people? We are looking for three people to take off round the world on a free six-month trip in November – and be Netjetters. Just send us 500 words on where you want to go, and why we should pick you.

My first thought was that this would be a good way of disposing of my unemployed son, who'd returned from college to clutter up my newly emptied nest. But a second impractical, impossible and idiotic idea wormed its way into my brain: why not apply myself? Five hundred words of frustrated travel ambition spilled onto the page within an hour.

I want to be a Netjetter. I am fifty, fairly fit and fed up. I am overworked, underpaid (public sector – worthy work, worthless pay) and impoverished by student offspring. I am ready to receive my reward in heaven – travelling.

That was me summed up in three sentences. Nothing of the trauma that followed the first midlife crisis: divorce after twenty-three years of marriage, a civilised parting of the ways that left me undamaged and unrepentant; a new career, swapping a craft shop for the Education Welfare Service (truant catching), and moving from the large family home to one half the size, minuscule but mine. Nothing of my three children's conspiracy to choose colleges in three different corners of the country, cramming the alphabet of student survival (TV, PC, VCR, DVD, CDs, a few clothes and even fewer books) into a Ford Fiesta. Nothing of the shock of my body reaching fifty, before my mind was ready.

I have long been consumed by the desire to travel. Pre-divorce, it was camping and car-sick children, with an occasional trip to France. It is one of life's small mysteries as to why all teachers are such Francophiles. In seven post-divorce years I have only managed three holidays: a first-time skiing trip to Italy, experiencing an equal measure of terror and exhilaration; a walking trip to Romania, feeling a curious mixture of envy and guilt at the simple but harsh peasant life, and a cheap week in Kefalonia, where the beauty of the island took my breath away every single day. I am currently saving for a trip to Nepal. At this rate I will have to live to the age of 150 to make a small dent on where I want to go.

I lied. There had been four holidays but I decided the judges didn't need to know about the Trappist week in Cyprus with a now ex-boyfriend; after a blazing row on the first day we didn't speak for the rest of the holiday.

My just-graduated son is also applying to be a Netjetter, but I say to him and all the young: sod off. He will have other chances. Which of us would be most excited by the adventure, most awestruck by the wonders of this planet, most appreciative of the diversity of its cultures?
I would consider it an honour to represent the Shirley Valentines and Bridget Joneses of this world. I would try my hardest to live up to all the dreams of middle-aged womankind – we are a feisty lot!

Since becoming single again, I've met so many courageous, adventurous women, but men like that remain hidden away in a place that I've not yet discovered.

Where do I want to go? EVERYWHERE AND ANYWHERE – definitely every continent. I do not know if a detailed itinerary is required. I can't be bothered to work that out now. It is too exciting just to think about the whole concept.

I will just throw out a few places high on my wish list: Prague, Krakow, St Petersburg, on to China, Nepal, into India, join the backpackers in Southeast Asia, pop to Australia and New Zealand, across to South America (any part will do but must include Peru), up to the Caribbean, I suppose I must include the States, if only to test out my long-held prejudices, Canada if time … I have just looked at an atlas and realised I have missed out Africa. I am sure I can fit it in somewhere.

The beauty of six months and a worldwide ticket would be the freedom to be side tracked, to be guided by other travellers and Guardian Unlimited readers, to go wherever the nose or the eyes led. My heart is beating so fast just thinking about it.

In the dusty atlas, the British Isles were a mere speck. Imagining myself wandering alone across the pages filled me with both ecstasy and terror.

I may not have a job to come back to. I would certainly have a lot of debts. It would be well worth it. I could live off the memories for the same amount of time it would take me to pay off the debts – probably the rest of my life. My family (apart from my son) and colleagues think I am mad to even apply – I probably am . . . but I can dream.

Job or trip? Security or adventure? No contest.

I want to be a Netjetter.

∞

The day the newspaper was due to notify the winners passed and the dream faded. It was two weeks later, when I was at work deep in the Fens, that Imogen from the Guardian Travel section rang. She said she was pleased to have finally tracked me down as my email wasn't working (so much for the County Council's brave new e-world). I'd been shortlisted to be a Netjetter, and could I come for an interview? I managed to stutter out that I would come to London on Friday. At the end of this brief conversation I was shaking, overcome by disbelief, excitement and panic. How close was I? Could I bear it if I failed the interview? Should I warn the boss? What do you wear to an interview for a trip around the world?

On Friday morning, having secured a day's leave, I set off for London. I'd considered impressing the panel with safari clothes, a sarong, sari or a friend of mine's Guatemalan national costume, but opted instead for 'casual' dress with a new pair of shoes. At the Guardian offices, I sat down with Imogen, Charlie and Sarah and let the thrill of the project carry me through. Asking why they'd picked me, I was told I was someone Guardian readers could identify with – an independent woman (divorced), public-sector worker (leftie) looking for something more from life (in midlife crisis. Did they know it was my second?).

Told to ring back at 4pm, I wandered the streets of London. My new shoes began to give me grief so I passed the interminable hours sitting in trendy bars, watching the Eye on its somniferous circle. By chance my three children were in London that weekend and I met my daughter Rachel outside the tube station, where with shaking hands, I tapped out the number. Engaged – be calm, try again – still engaged. How could they do this to me? Finally Imogen answered with the news that I was to be a Netjetter.

The commuters looked warily at the two generations of women dancing around and laughing hysterically.

∞

The departure date of December 1st gave me just seven

weeks to reorganise my life. The first hurdle was facing my boss, who, after a few expletives, consulted with those on high and granted me a six-month unpaid sabbatical. The second hurdle was choosing my route, so I set off to London again to meet the competition sponsors, the travel company Bridge the World.

It was October 19th, the day after my fifty-first birthday. How different from my last birthday, when turning fifty had seemed a gigantic step down a steep slope. The 20/20 vision had already gone, I'd slipped into the second ladies' tennis team and sex was a distant memory. A year later the fifties didn't seem so bad as I sat opposite Christian, my travel consultant, with a map of the world between us.

Negotiations began:

'No, you can't exchange a flight for the Trans-Siberian Railway.'

'Sorry, BA/Qantas don't fly to Nepal.'

'Australia is compulsory.'

'You've run out of air miles mid-Pacific. Let's try again…'

And so it progressed until I'd squeezed in as many stops as possible (eleven) and used every mile available (28,000). The end result was London to Mumbai (Bombay), to Singapore and Malaysia, on to Bali, then Darwin and across to Sydney, over to Auckland, across to Buenos Aires, Santiago, overland to Peru and back from Lima with a stop at Barcelona. Wow! Sadly Africa had to be crossed off in favour of South America, as there weren't enough miles for both.

What was to happen when I arrived in these places was, as yet, a total mystery, but I did know that with only the flights included in the prize, I had to become a backpacker. In keeping with my new Guardian persona, I also wanted to travel ethically, using local resources and having as little impact as possible on the environment. This was only a wishy-washy ideal at that moment and I'd little idea what it would mean in practice.

My route determined, I visited the travel clinic to discover that I needed every jab available, which had to be administered in batches as there was so little time. Despite the holes in my sore arms, I felt well enough to carry on with the new 'fitness regime': running up and down the stairs. Starting from a very poor six times up and down, I reached the giddy total of sixteen by week five. It was fortunate that no one saw me after this exercise; I was a sorry figure gasping for breath, tottering on jelly legs as far as the sofa before reaching for the fag packet. Besides travel, my life's ambition was to give up smoking. Here was my perfect opportunity to give up – once I set off, of course.

The Guardian arranged another meeting with all three Netjetters and it wasn't too difficult to work out that I was to be the 'oldie' even before I met twenty-nine-year-old Sam and eighteen-year-old Milly. Sam was quiet and reflective, a civil servant anxious to escape London and his job. Millie was in her post-A level gap year, lively and scatty. The deal was to email back a weekly diary with photographs onto an interactive website, and we went through email addresses, passwords, contracts, contacts, etc. I decided not to tell them that I'd only had a computer at work for two weeks, didn't know what an internet café looked like (much less what you did in one) and that I'd never seen a digital camera before.

That seemed to be all the nitty-gritty sorted, so I moved on to the Indian High Commission for a visa. The building looked closed but, short of leave to make another journey to London, I slipped through a side door that was slightly ajar. The door locked itself behind me with an ominous clunk and I was trapped in a small lobby, feeling like Susan in Wonderland. My white rabbit was an official, who eventually spotted me, confirmed that they were shut for a festival and let me out.

Was this a warning of how the next six months were going to be? Never terribly organised, famed for mislaying either my bag, glasses, an important piece of paper or all three at once, many of my colleagues wondered openly how I was going to manage six months around the world. I didn't tell them about this episode, or the Sunday visit to my office to use the internet, when I forgot to put the door to the toilets on the latch and locked myself out from access to telephone, keys, alarms and exits. After a period of despair in which I envisaged having to bed down in the loo until I was rescued in the morning, I managed to climb out of a tiny window, bending my body at painful angles until at last it all squeezed through.

Money was a major anxiety, but the young man in the bank was quite excited when I explained why I needed a loan. He assured me that I could have as much as I wanted – with my house as security, of course. Discarding the post-divorce vow to live without credit, I rejoined the age of plastic but, unsure of the existence of cash machines in jungles and up mountains, I decided to take my spending money in US dollar traveller's cheques. I now had $7,000 in traveller's cheques and $1,386 in cash – the equivalent of £6,000 in ready money, plus the card. I had no idea whether £1,000 a month was a realistic amount, but it was a nice easy sum to hang on to.

Sam was well into his adult life in London, Rachel had just started college in Devon and Ben was still 'resting' at home. They were not really a worry but income to cover ongoing bills was. Word spread that there might be lodgings going at the Stubbings' house, and two of my son's mates presented themselves for inspection. Dave asked all sorts of sensible questions like 'Where is the stopcock?' and Mark was happy to feed the cats, so a deal was struck.

As the weeks rushed by, it was time to think about packing. How do you know what you are going to need for six months in strange places, and how do you carry it without resembling a mutant snail? My one concession to age and a dodgy back was a rucksack with wheels. The pile of all-purpose, all-weather, all-culture basic items of clothing was, in fact, smaller than that of the purchases from Boots' pharmaceutical counter.

My major dilemma was shoes. Walking boots and walking sandals were a must, but should I take one pair of smarter shoes? They were put on the pile then taken away, put back, replaced by trainers, then put back plus the trainers. After the first attempt at fitting everything in the bag, smart shoes and trainers were dispatched to the attic.

I wasn't sure if it was against the competition rules but I'd gained a travelling companion: Bruce, a teddy bear, belonged to Class 6 at Highfield School for children with learning difficulties. The class had agreed that Bruce, an experienced traveller, could go on a special assignment for six months as my companion and bodyguard. I was very touched and knew I'd be glad of the company.

By the last week I was exhausted and, at this time of emotional goodbyes to family, friends and colleagues, the doubts and worries finally surfaced. What did I think I was doing heading off round the world at fifty-one, never having been outside Europe, never having backpacked, never having travelled alone before? How would the children manage without me? What if I ran out of money? What on earth do you do once you arrive at an airport? With no time to do any research, it was all going to be seat-of-the-pants. What had I let myself in for?

At 8.30am on Friday, December 1st, I walked through the departure gate at Heathrow, stomach churning. Too late to turn back now – this was it, for better or for worse. The adventure had begun.

2

Don't you worry 'bout a thing, Mama

I'd only travelled from my son Sam's flat in London but, by the time I reached the check-in desk at Heathrow, I was exhausted. A sleepless night, the emotional goodbyes to my children and the need to visit the toilet every ten minutes were compounded by the bruising battle of wills with my unwieldy rucksack, whose wheels put the most perverse supermarket trolley to shame. Heaving it on to the black conveyor belt, relief turned to anxiety as the long tongues of plastic swallowed it up. Would I ever see it again? Would it survive all the wear and tear of what lay ahead? We were in this together, me and my rucksack, mutually dependent for the next six months. The third part of my team, Bruce the teddy bear, remained safely tucked up in my hand luggage among the snacks, novel, book of crosswords and nicotine chewing gum – survival equipment for the nine-hour flight.

At 10.20am the plane took off for Mumbai, my first long-haul flight, my first trip outside Europe, on the first of the 183 days that stretched ahead. What would each one bring? By day twenty or day forty or day one hundred and eighty would I be home, in hospital, a hostage, hungry, homesick or hung-over? Of one thing I was certain: unless forced by my legs falling off or the outbreak of World War III, I would see it through to the end.

For the first time since winning the prize, I asked myself what I wanted from this trip. Married at twenty, three children by thirty-two, my only big risk in life had been getting divorced

17

at forty-three. I wanted to experience the world for sure, but more than that it was time to find out what this rather shy, ordinary middle-aged woman was made of.

Between musing and shuffling around the plane every hour or so, I chatted to Margaret and Harry in the adjoining seats. Seasoned, organised travellers, familiar with both India and South America, they seemed surprised both at my lack of experience of travelling and the absence of any research on where I was going. The manic weeks between winning the prize and leaving had been filled with reorganising my entire life; there was no time left for the luxury of leafing through guidebooks or learning 'hello' in Hindi, Balinese and Spanish. My sole piece of forward planning had been to book myself onto a three-week overland trip with the Imaginative Traveller tour company through Rajasthan into Nepal, a necessity to assuage the terror of starting the trip in India. I convinced myself that being a novice traveller gave me the dubious advantage of arriving in a country with very few preconceptions. Any impressions of India came from the screen: Gandhi, A Passage to India and The Jewel in the Crown.

Due either to a surfeit of aspirin or emotional shutdown, Margaret and Harry's warnings of beggars, smells and toilets passed me by, as did the bumpy landing at midnight. I ambled down the exit ramp, breezed through all the official bits and glided to the baggage collection area, where my bag was one of the first to judder down the ramp with its assorted locks, coloured straps and back-saving wheels intact. We trundled down a corridor, which was deserted as the taxi, accommodation and money-changing stalls were all shut for the night.

Turning the corner into the arrivals area it was as if a switch had been thrown, transforming order, quiet and air-conditioning into a wall of noise, heat and mayhem, rudely waking me from my disembodied calm. A bellowing throng of taxi wallahs, hotel touts, drivers waving scrawled names and excited relatives pressed against the barrier, exuding a pungent fug that hit the nose and ears like a mallet.

I froze, cowering against a wall, expecting this human river to breach the flimsy rope that held it at bay and drown me. It was only when I spotted the Imaginative Traveller logo being waggled deep in the crowd that a surge of adrenaline enabled me to goad the jelly-legs into action. Putting my head down, I charged towards this beacon of hope, not caring how many bare ankles and sandalled feet my bag crushed behind me. The small white-suited Indian attached to the sign seemed to accept that we were meant for each other and purposefully guided me through the crowd to a white van. I was too exhausted to consider any alternatives and obediently followed.

As the driver spoke no English and I no Hindi, my introduction to Indian traffic took place in silence – just as well, as it took all my concentration not to scream as we careered our way into the city. The streets criss-crossed like elongated dodgem rides through which my driver, one hand on the wheel and the other on the horn, zig-zagged at high speed, weaving into any gap that appeared in the lane-less anarchy. As we missed motorised rickshaws and large chrome lorries by millimetres, I was convinced that this first night was going to be my last. Holding my head at ninety degrees so I wouldn't see death approaching, I stared instead at the vast numbers of people sleeping on the streets, the long rows of bodies resembling the shrouded aftermath of some terrible disaster.

Arriving at the hotel at 1.30am, my driver hovered expectantly but, not yet having any rupees and by now totally witless, it didn't occur to me just to give him a dollar. I expect he cursed all English women with big bags, as a night's work had only earned him the pittance from the hotel. Too exhausted to sort out the tight layers of the enormous bed, I crawled into my cotton sleeping sheet on top of the covers and instantly fell asleep.

∞

In the morning, the shower dial proved to be as baffling as the bed, but the ice-cold dunking had the effect of wakening my fuzzy brain to the fact that I was actually in India. Sitting on the big double bed in my room, in this huge city, in this enormous continent, I was terrified at the thought of leaving this safe room. After busying myself re-packing my bag, ordering coffee, changing money, re-re-packing the bag and ordering more coffee, I needed company. Talking to a rucksack was bordering on insanity, so it had to be Bruce:

'Well, little teddy bear, am I really going to cry on day two?'

Either I got on with it or spent the rest of my life avoiding all Guardian readers. Popping Bruce into my day sack, I squared my shoulders and crossed the hotel threshold – one giant step for middle-aged womankind.

Outside was an array of yellow, motorised rickshaw taxis. An affable driver shouted at me. 'Forty rupees to the Gateway.'

'Thirty,' I replied.

The driver waggled his head in agreement. Done.

Pleased with my first attempt at bargaining, I stepped into the rickshaw adorned with a Bollywood Elvis look-alike. We were off, out into the maelstrom, twice as busy and twice as scary as the previous night, the daylight affording even more opportunities for vehicles to cut each other up. The squeaky horns of the rickshaws provided a staccato accompaniment to the bass of the lorries. Diesel fumes hung in the air, so thick you could scoop up them up in handfuls. Last night's shrouded bodies had been resurrected as ice sellers, holy men, beggars and shoe-shine boys, a human market clamouring for trade amongst the stalls of rainbow-coloured bangles, elaborate jewellery, religious paraphernalia, spices and exotic fruit and vegetables. I watched an ear cleaner brandishing a long, lethal-looking skewer in an ear, but we drove past before I could see if it reappeared out of the other side.

The taxi driver dropped me near the Gateway, a hundred-foot ornate brick arch overlooking the sea. As they spotted me the waiting crowd rippled and I felt like Michael Caine facing the Zulu hordes, the red coat replaced by a sign on my head saying 'New tourist, alone and scared.' Every tout, guide, holy man, taxi driver, beggar and ticket seller rushed towards me and within minutes I'd bought a useless map for a ridiculous price and was clutching a handful of holy grain while red and yellow sacred thread was deftly tied round my wrist. I searched for an escape route, certain that if I stayed here I would lose not only all my money but my precarious nerve.

Given the choice between drowning in this mêlée or in the sea, I jumped on a boat for the hour-long trip to Elephanta Island. To a collective groan from the disappointed throng on the quayside, I watched Mumbai recede. By the time we reached the island, my panic had subsided sufficiently for me to enjoy the little train ride up through woodland to caves full of ancient carvings, but not enough for me to face the queue to go in. I sat outside in the sun watching the monkeys forage for food scraps, ignoring a group of grumbling German and French students who'd taken offence that the entry fee was $10 for foreigners and only 10 rupees for Indians, or 1/45th of the price for tourists. Despite the fierce heat, I walked back down the stony path to the boat, the exercise and a good sweat restoring enough equilibrium for me to return to the city to face the next challenge: food.

In an unpretentious restaurant devoid of tourists, and amid the curious stares of the predominantly male clientele, I asked for beer and a biryani. The waiter, with a sad apologetic shrug, told me, 'No beer, Muslim, but beer down road,' his manner suggesting it was entirely his fault, not mine. With my face tandoori-red, I drank my Coke and picked at the food, wondering how you could tell Muslim from Hindu.

It was now time to lose my cyber-virginity and venture into an internet café. My only research into these alien establishments had been to look in the window of Cambridge's CB1, a cosy coffee house lined with books, with a room at the back full of bespectacled students hunched over computers. The Mumbai version had no armchairs, only tiny booths with a computer and metal chair, no coffee, no conversation, and

21

no time to waste, as time was money. A young girl set my machine on Hotmail and I was away, writing my first report back, a rather short account of my first day that the Guardian titled Bewildered in Bombay.

Tired, I headed back to the hotel in a proper-car taxi that went round in what even I recognised as circles as the same one-armed child accosted us three times. In just one day I'd seen many of these casualties of birth or circumstance, and although pre-warned that giving money perpetuates begging by gangs with unscrupulous pimps, it wasn't easy to ignore the children's big eyes, skinny bodies and missing limbs. Just as upsetting were the women, often little more than children themselves, who thrust babies at me, asking for money for milk. Most poignant were the toothless old women, abandoned with no family to take them in, who sat on the ground holding out their tin cups in silent resignation.

Eventually the driver got out to ask directions, locking me in the car. Too tired to worry, I was just sitting still when a young boy started banging on the window asking for water. Deeply shocked by his deformed face, with the mouth and little hamster teeth twisted round away from his nose and eyes, I don't know why I didn't just give him my water bottle. It was as if by opening the window I would let in a flood that would drown me.

Throughout this first twenty-four hours, every sense had been assaulted by the sights, sounds and smells of Mumbai; my emotions, normally well under control, had been dragged out of their comfort zone. Sitting in this taxi, I felt totally overwhelmed by India, by the enormity of what I was undertaking and by the fact that I was on my own, so far from home and anything familiar.

The driver returned, shooed the boy away and drove straight to the hotel. Although it was only 9pm, I crawled into my sheet, exhausted.

∞

Eleven hours' sleep and the knowledge that I was to hand

myself over to a competent tour leader made the second morning very different. Today I felt excitement rather than dread as I waited in the foyer, ready to meet my companions for the next three weeks.

Carol, the tour leader, arrived first, irrepressibly cheerful and bouncy. Like many reps, she'd set off travelling on her own and had just kept going. It was an exciting and challenging but also a rootless life and, in her mid-thirties, Carol had lasted longer than most.

A couple from New Zealand were the next to arrive. Claire, a lawyer, was tall and thin, with a dry sense of humour and a nasty bug picked up in the Gambia, where they'd been the week before. Her fiancé, Mike, a food technician who'd spent the last year making Wotsits in Wales, was over six feet tall and nearly as wide, very jolly despite a bad cold.

We were a select band of only four. As we travelled through India, big Mike in his red Welsh rugby shirt, with his harem of three women, was the centre of attention; his attraction was enhanced by a love of cricket that enabled him to happily talk googlies and silly-mid-offs with any locals, a necessary social skill here. His size was a problem when the three of us squashed into one rickshaw to go into the city for the afternoon, but a blessing when I became detached and spotted Mike's head above the dense crowd.

Carol and I were to share a room for the three weeks of the tour and I was taken aback when, on the first night, I found her demolishing a plate of chips while surfing the TV channels.

'This is my sixth week on tour and there is only so much curry that an English body can take,' she explained.

I learned to live with her addiction to television and she with mine to nicotine.

∞

The tour started in earnest at 4.30am the next morning with a train journey to Ahmedabad in the province of Gujarat, three hundred miles north of Mumbai, our stepping stone to the journey proper through Rajasthan. With no idea what to expect on my first Indian train ride, the station was a shock as I surveyed the prone bundles of rags that gradually mutated into human beings as the homeless and poor roused themselves for the coming day.

When we finally boarded, a continuous jangling made me wonder if this was a convict train full of shackled prisoners, but it was merely the cumulative sound of gold chains and bangles wobbling on chubby necks, ankles and arms. This was first-class travel, comfortable with face-to-face rows of seats, but uninspiring as the windows were all frosted. After visiting the 'superior' squat loos I was relieved that we weren't in economy class, as I couldn't imagine the horrors of an 'inferior' loo.

I spent the nine hours reading the instructions for my new digital camera, irritating Claire and Mike by continuously interrupting their intense study of the guidebook to try out a shot. At this time digital cameras were quite new and the Guardian had decided that to be able to send back photos, we should be given ones that used floppy discs. This rather bulky Sony camera took great shots and the ability to show the picture on the back screen was a great hit all round the world, especially with children.

Although Ahmedabad was a more open and spacious city than Mumbai, the traffic was worse. Cars and motorised rickshaws were outnumbered by solid streams of scooter riders and cyclists, all with loud horns and a death wish. Our brief stop included a visit to the Calico Museum of Textiles, where we acquired a demented guide who rushed us round the exhibits.

'Keep up,' she screeched, staring at us with manic eyes before scuttling off into the next room.

Mike leaned forward to inspect a piece of Rajasthani embroidery.

'No touch!' the guide roared. 'Come on.'

We panted breathlessly after her from room to room. After two days of streets full of women in bright saris I already felt like Plain Jane in my Western clothes, but here

I was the fashion equivalent of magnolia paint compared to the beautiful magenta and peacock-green saris embroidered with gold. Enormous deep-red wall hangings depicting tales of Krishna hung from the ceilings; orange, blue and gold cloth with little woven-in mirrors graced the walls, and a royal tent embroidered with every colour of the rainbow gave camping a new dimension.

After a visit to the peaceful gardens of Gandhi's ashram, where sweeping lawns offered quiet tree-shaded areas for contemplation, Carol walked us to her favourite restaurant. I was unnerved by the locals stopping to look at us, knowing it couldn't be because of the vibrancy of our clothes.

'Why is everybody staring?' I asked.

'Well it's not me,' said Mike. 'I've checked my flies twice already.'

'It's fine,' Carol assured us. 'They don't see many visitors around here and anyway, staring isn't considered rude in Asia.'

Relaxing, I grinned at a toddler shyly peeking from behind his mother's sari. The results were dramatic as the woman smiled back, lifting the toddler for me to admire. We then beamed at everyone so much that a crowd gathered, keen to communicate with these strangely-dressed and oddly-shaped foreigners. Few tourists meant fewer beggars and aggressive touts, which was a relief, although I wasn't too keen on having my hand seized by several women who said it would bring them luck. But I was to remember the value of a smile for the rest of the trip.

∞

After our brief experience of Gujarati trains, for the next two weeks we were to explore Rajasthan by car. The next morning we found our driver, Manesh, leaning nonchalantly against the bonnet of a station wagon. Leather jacket on despite the searing heat, hair sleeked back and with black shades and an inscrutable expression, he was obviously ready for the day that a talent scout from Bollywood (or perhaps even Hollywood) would be amongst his passengers. As we drove one hundred and fifty miles northeast into the dry hinterland of India, the traffic thinned, the drivers calmed down and more cows, camels, pigs and assorted wildfowl joined us on the dusty roads.

We followed the hippie trail of the 1960s to Udaipur, a city of white marble buildings built on the banks of Lake Pichola; to Pushkar, a holy city of four hundred temples and fifty-two ghats – steps leading down to bathing areas in holy rivers – and on to Jaisalmer, where most of the city lay within a fort protected by high, sheer sandstone ramparts. These towns were a world apart from the urban sprawl of Mumbai and Ahmedabad as they were packed with impressive royal buildings, temples, gardens and forts.

In Udaipur we explored the enormous City Palace, a museum, hotel and home of the current maharani (maharaja's wife), where every granite or marble wall was covered in miniature religious paintings of Hindu mythology. These, together with the stained glass windows and peacock glass mosaics, made the whole building glow with coloured light. Next door was the Jagdish Temple, built of carved white marble and with little shrines built into the main temple platform.

The Sahelion-ki-Bari, or Garden of Maidens, was where the women of the court came to wander round the peaceful gardens dominated by four lily-filled pools decorated with fountains and stone elephants. We all 'oohed' in amazement when our guide clapped his hands and the fountains leapt into action, pretending that we hadn't seen the boy turning a handle behind a bush. In the nearby town of Ahar was a complex of royal cenotaphs representing the rulers of Mewar. The size, variety and complexity of these monuments – ornate pavilions housing statues of gods and mythical beasts – was so impressive that it was hard to believe that our quartet and two buffalo were the only visitors.

I wandered on my own through the streets of Udaipur, eating snacks from stalls in the market. Then I took tea in one of the sumptuous hotels beside the lake, very high tea with silver teapot, china cups and English cakes, served by a turbaned waiter in a dazzlingly white jacket. The initial terror of that first twenty-four hours in Mumbai was melting away and I was beginning to enjoy myself and appreciate the beauty of this land. Away from the polluted cities, the light in India was clear and sharp and the sky blue in the day, surrendering to the night in a blaze of colour.

From the Monsoon Palace on a hill four hundred metres above the city I witnessed my first Indian sunset, bathing the city and nearby lake in pink and purple light. Returning from the island of Jag Mandir after admiring the gardens and yet more large stone elephants, my second sunset experience was on a boat in the middle of Lake Pichola. The sun set over the city, silhouetting the exotic skyline of turreted palaces, pointed domes and the white marble Lake Palace Hotel, built on an island in the lake. How far I felt from the flat fens of East Anglia.

∞

Occasionally, I have wondered where all the dreadlocked folk go after Glastonbury. As we wandered the streets of Pushkar, where stalls of religious memorabilia and orange blossoms vied with those sporting tie-dyed T-shirts and wind chimes, I saw that they were here in the cafés of Pushkar enjoying the local brew, yoghurt laced with cannabis known as bangh lassi.

'I would just like to say,' announced Carol in her responsible tour-guide voice, 'that I strongly advise you to stick to banana lassi.'

'Why?' I asked.

'Because I don't wish to find you wandering the streets of Pushkar at two in the morning chasing pink elephants and shouting at flying camels.'

'That sounds like the voice of experience.'

Carol didn't elaborate but marched us off on a two-hour hike up a hill to the temple of Savitri. At the top, as we were enjoying our reward of another rose sunset, a chai wallah materialised out of the masonry beside us, with his blackened pot steaming over a stove. After the sweet, spicy tea had been almost boiled to nothing, it was strained into a little clay dish for us to drink. I cast a nervous glance at the chai wallah when Carol smashed her empty dish on the ground but his inscrutable expression never changed, as apparently this was the custom – one of the few concessions to hygiene on the streets of India.

The pot and the man compared unfavourably with the china teapots and turbaned waiters of Udaipur but I happily drank my first chai, confident that no form of life could survive all that boiling. The same couldn't be said for the lunch in Pushkar that gave Mike and Claire their first bout of 'Delhi belly'. They admitted they should have left after the waiter wiped the plates on the curtains.

On the way back to our hotel, the sound of pipes and cymbals drew us to a Hindu wedding procession. The groom, resplendent in a white embroidered suit, sat on a white horse covered in lavishly decorated cloths and plumes. The family followed in their multi-coloured finery, accompanied by musicians and dancers in a noisy, joyful procession. I felt sure the waiting bride would be impressed by this handsome figure sitting ramrod-straight on an equally handsome beast.

My mind wandered back to my own wedding, a happy occasion with some colour from the fluffy bridesmaids and mothers' hats, but corseted within the formal stiffness of two families on their best behaviour. I tried to imagine my ex-in-laws and assorted kith and kin dancing through the streets beating drums and cymbals, but failed. Would this marriage, presumably arranged between the families, stand any less chance of being successful than my own?

I had married for love, a burning emotion that had made my chest hurt, but here I was thirty years later watching this procession alone. My bright flame had died with the changing years; I wondered if it might be better to start with a tiny spark and work at nurturing it rather than follow my example. I didn't mention this to Claire and Mike, who were planning to marry the following year.

Pushkar, an important pilgrimage centre, was my first chance to send my meagre stock of clothes to the laundry. I felt a disproportionate pleasure at seeing my little pile of underwear and T-shirts come back all clean again, but I swear that everything was a shade paler. Had my clothes been down to the river to be beaten on rocks, as I had seen the women doing? In contrast, my body took on rainbow streaks as, wandering down to the ghats, I was trapped by a holy man who thrust an orange flower in my hand and began to bless my family.

'May your mother and father live long and happy lives,' he mumbled.

'Sorry, too late, they're both dead.'

'May they rest in peace. But your children, how many?'

'Three but I have to go, I'm meeting...' I answered distractedly while searching for an escape route.

'May your blessed children have full and long lives,' he interrupted. 'And how many brothers and sisters do you have?'

At this point I decided enough was enough and paid the price of freedom, which was yet another sacred string round my wrist. This wasn't the last adornment, though. Coming out of the Brahma temple, I was grabbed by a tiny, wrinkled old lady with a face resembling a raisin, who piped brown prune juice on my hand. Despite my protests, the spider's web spread ever more intricately across my palm, which was trapped in her vice-like grip. Surrendering, I let her finish, paying half of what she asked and then frantically tried to wipe it off. I succeeded only in ruining a top and irrevocably staining my bag. In the shower later that day, the dye from the string covered me in red and yellow streaks which, together with the henna, lasted several weeks, giving me a daily reminder of Pushkar.

∞

During the eight-hour drive to Jaisalmer the next day, Carol passed the time by giving us our first 'lesson' on Indian religions. When she tired of it herself and had a snooze, I listened to the music tapes that my children had compiled for me. They had conferred, so there was no repetition, but Ben is such a perfectionist that there wasn't any hesitation or deviation either. His offering, 'Eclectjetter', was a compilation that included the Stevie Wonder song Don't you worry 'bout a thing. Hearing Stevie tell his mumma not to worry about the changes in her life as he would be standing in the wings, my throat tightened and I hastily put on my sunglasses, emotional at this message from my son. Truthfully, though I thought about my children often and worried about the parties that were inevitably happening in my house, as yet I felt little homesickness – travelling was too new and exciting. With a smile at the song, I too dropped off to sleep.

A couple of hours later, Manesh roused us in time to watch a fairy-tale golden fort rise out of the desert ahead like a giant sandcastle. Within its golden walls, pitted by erosion from the desert wind and antiquated drainage, was a maze of narrow cobbled lanes lined with multi-coloured shops and stalls. The temples, mansions, hotels and guesthouses were built of the same warm stone or mellow wood and were embellished with carved filigree, making the city look and feel truly ancient. After losing the others in the criss-cross of tiny alleys, I had to squash myself flat against a wall to let a fat cow coming in the opposite direction lumber past. When level with me, it lifted its tail; I wondered if being splashed by sacred cow wee was a blessing.

At the city museum, after venturing up several narrow winding staircases, I found myself on a large flat roof above the city, looking down on the wide ramparts and the jumble of buildings below and out over the rocky desert, with distant brown hills poking into the cloudless blue sky.

Alone in my rooftop lookout, soaking up the sun and savouring the views, the full force of my good fortune hit me. It was chance that had brought me here. I rarely bought a newspaper, so seeing the competition at all was the first stroke of luck. By rights, I should be at work berating parents for their children's poor school attendance.

The unlucky few who came my way in Cambridgeshire were a drop in the world's oceans compared to the children here, many of whom scavenged the streets or hassled tourists instead of going to school. At first I was charmed by smiling children asking 'Where are you from?' but as any reply other than London or Manchester (of United fame) drew a blank, and every child tried to persuade me to visit either their father, uncle, brother or cousin's shop, the novelty soon wore off.

In the evening we went to watch a traditional puppet show at the Desert Cultural Museum. In the foyer sat a gentleman in flowing white robes and a magenta turban. His demeanour and corpulent frame suggested this was no ordinary mortal, and the immaculately manicured curly moustache that spread across his chubby cheeks like two ferrets was the final clue. It was the local maharaja, who graced the foyer most evenings as a gesture of support for the museum. To have a real maharaja thrown in made the entry fee a bargain.

The puppets, dangling from strings worked by men in white shifts, told stories of dancing princesses, forlorn lovers and a dashing swordsman who could slip under the belly of his horse to elude his enemies. We tried hard to stifle our giggles, unsure if the puppets were meant to be comic, but the dancing camel with whirling legs convinced us that it was OK to laugh.

The owner, Mr Shah, had a mission to preserve this ancient art form, and trained impoverished local villagers to work the puppets. He was excited when I asked to take a photograph and gave him a card with my website address. The show, the setting, the puppets and stories were full of charm, wit and a timeless innocence that made it a memorable evening.

Later at the 4th July Restaurant, the affable German host explained the significance of the name and took orders. 'My wife's birthday. Good name, ja? What would you like?'

'Oh no, not again,' interrupted Mike. 'Where's the bathroom?'

"A lassi for me and a Coke for his wayward stomach, please,' said Claire, ordering for the absent Mike.

'Nein, nein, nein,' said our host wagging a fat finger that resembled a German sausage. 'Coke no good, he must have my special, guaranteed to cure all Delhi bellies. It is famous here with all delicate travellers.'

When Mike reappeared, he looked askance at the dish of yoghurt and muesli.

'You must eat only this today and return for the same tomorrow morning.'

Mike reluctantly did as he was told and watched us tucking into curry, the green of his gills matching the envy in his eyes. I had turned vegetarian in India but there was a wide choice of curries full of flavour rather than heat. My favourites were a curry sauce with a boiled egg and the cheesy panir curries.

∞

Obediently returning to the 4th July the next morning for more belly-settling yoghurt obviously worked its magic, as Mike resumed his cheerful banter when we set out for the much-anticipated camel safari.

An hour out of Jaisalmer by bumpy jeep, we met our transport for the day. The sight of big Mike climbing out of the jeep caused the camel wallahs to hold a huddled conference before leading him to the largest, sturdiest beast. As they fussed over their camel and Mike, we women were left to choose our own animals. I looked into all the camels' doleful eyes in turn but received no signal saying, 'Pick me, oh Englishwoman,' so chose the one with the least flies around his nose and a pretty blue flowery seat.

When I asked what his name was, the camel man uttered a guttural, 'Drrrrr.' Ignoring the possibility that he was taking the piss, I climbed aboard Drrrrr, who was kneeling obediently on the ground. As he unfolded his gangly legs to stand up, it was a close call as to which end I would slither off but I managed to cling on and, once Drrrrr was stabilised, settled comfortably on my high perch.

Besides being very big and smelling of overflowing dustbins mixed with wet wool, Drrrrr was also very greedy.

He stopped at every clump of coarse grass to tear off great mouthfuls, refusing to budge until every blade had been thoroughly ruminated in exaggerated, sideways chews. As the others forged ahead, I clicked my tongue, pleaded, banged my knees against his sides, pulled (not too hard) at the rope attached to the spike through his nose, even resorted to abuse, but I just couldn't make him move. My inadequacy as a camel rider was exposed time and again as various camel men had to backtrack to restart Drrrrr with a mere swish of a rope.

Despite my stop-start progress, I was enjoying ambling through the bright yellow sand, breathing the clean desert air, not a tout, beggar or rickshaw for miles. The desert itself was silent but the camels provided a continuous soundtrack of desert battles – Gatling guns of farting and artillery barrages of dung thudding into the sand.

It was relatively smooth going until we reached the dunes where, after trudging up the steep slopes, diffident Drrrrr suddenly changed personality. Like a child at the first snowfall, he became juvenile, launching himself down the dune at terrifying speed. As my backside slithered dangerously right, left and backwards, all animal-welfare considerations were discarded as I tugged on the nose-rope for dear life in an effort to slow the headlong descent.

The whoops and screams of the others told me that it wasn't only Drrrrr who was behaving badly and endangering the life of his passenger. Shaken but not unseated, we all arrived safely at the bottom, rubbing the various areas that had been burnt by the friction or clenched too hard in the effort to remain on board. Mike, in particular, jiggled uncomfortably, trying not to let on how much distress certain parts of his anatomy were in. The camel men, barely hiding their smirks, belatedly told us that we had to keep the camel's head high and the rein very short when descending.

Slightly saddle-sore, we reached our destination, Sunset Point, where the camel trains gathered in the late afternoon. A young lad, laden down with Coke in a basket of ice, ran barefoot beside us until we finally stopped and dismounted.

His reward was the sale of four bottles and he settled down beside us to watch the sun setting. Though free of tummy troubles, I'd acquired a streaming cold and blamed Mike, who acknowledged his guilt by crying, 'Bless you, sorry,' every time I sneezed. My nose was in full flow and I gave it an almighty blow into a handful of tissues before putting the soggy bundle into my pocket.

'Ugh!' said the boy, in an involuntary expression of disgust, looking at me as if I had just smeared myself with camel dung. Carol, Mike and Claire laughed so much that they ended up rolling all the way down the dune. Faced with this baffling Western behaviour, the poor lad was confused and worried. For my part, it was a salutary lesson in not judging cultural differences. However, I still couldn't bring myself to blow onto the ground as the Indians do and continued with my revolting practice of walking about with a pocket full of mucus.

When the last of the red rays disappeared below the dunes of the Thar Desert, we headed for our campsite. The blue-and-orange stripy tents were already up and the crew was busy cooking our dinner of curried vegetables. Sitting on rugs around a campfire, drinking beer in the middle of the desert, was a fitting end to a good day. I was feeling decidedly rough from my cold but Mike had yet more troubles when he discovered that his camel had off-loaded one of its ticks into his leg. Immediately reverting to small boy mode, he reminded me of my son Ben who, when his first milk tooth fell out, stood in the middle of Cambridge screaming that he was going to die. The patient camel man assured Mike that it wasn't fatal and that once blasted with sun cream, it could be pulled out the next day.

Mike still checked every five minutes. 'Are you sure my leg's not going to drop off?'

'No, leg good.'

Not convinced, Mike limped off to bed looking pale and anxious.

∞

I woke at about 2am and sought a suitable bush. The moonlight covered the desert with a ghostly silver glow, bright enough to silhouette the dunes, sparse trees and tents. This was my first experience of desert and I felt drawn to the austere beauty and the seductive silence that calmed the mind and body, removing any need for words or even thoughts that might disturb the quiet. I sat away from the tents under the moon, savouring my surroundings until the sharp cold drove me back under the covers. What seemed like minutes later, I was woken for breakfast, which we ate as the pale pink dawn spread over the sky and the desert.

It was time now for the ceremonial removal of the expired tick. An expectant hush fell over the small crowd of trekkers and camel men as Carol laid out her instruments on a clean towel.

'Cotton wool!' she barked, breaking the tense silence. 'Antiseptic cream! Tweezers!'

We held our breath.

'Got the bugger!' she exclaimed in triumph, holding up what looked like a tiny wizened mouse dropping. What an anticlimax – no blood, no gore, no glory for the ashen Mike, who looked crestfallen when Carol insisted that his leg really didn't need a splint. She tried to cheer him up by agreeing to a sticky plaster.

I could quite happily have stayed longer in the desert but tour schedules were tight and it was time to say goodbye to Drrrrr. I felt we'd bonded in our short time together but I wouldn't forget him quickly, as his odour lingered on my clothes for weeks.

∞

We spent three more days on the dusty roads of Rajasthan, stopping first at Jodhpur, with its buildings covered in a blue wash (originally, we were told, to deter termites), and then the pink city of Jaipur, painted to welcome the Prince of Wales in the 19th century.

We were travelling so far and so fast to so many hilltop

forts and palace museums that only particularly interesting features now caught our imagination. The huge Meherangarh Fort, hacked out of the mountainside, cast a brooding shadow over the city of Jodhpur. At the gates of the fort were the handprints of the widows of the Maharaja who, in 1843, defied British law by throwing themselves on their husband's funeral pyre; it was an action that was incomprehensible to me, a woman who'd thrown a small party when her divorce papers came through.

In Jaipur, the pinkest of all the buildings was the Palace of Winds, a fan-shaped five-storey building with 593 screened windows where the women of the court, in purdah, could look out over the city. What a life, to be shut away, sharing your man with dozens of others. Not only that but when he died, probably of exhaustion, there was the choice of his funeral pyre or a beggar's tin cup.

More memorable than the marble carving of the Amber Fort at Jaipur was the elephant ride up the path to the gates. Our beast, No 96, was the smallest one there and bellowed loudly on the steep path when our little band had trouble distributing its many kilos evenly in the cramped howdah perched on its back.

Everywhere, the wealth and splendour of these Rajasthani hilltop palaces and forts contrasted powerfully with the poverty and squalor in the cities below. Scabby dogs, ragged children, beggars, chickens, vendors, bristly boars, large cows and ordinary citizens thronged the streets. The dirt, dung and piles of rubbish remained where they fell, to be picked at by the scavenging animals. The sight of a cow munching its way through a large piece of cardboard soon ceased to surprise me.

I was also getting used to the smell of India, a mixture of refuse, spicy food and urine, and I no longer bothered to avert my eyes as men peed in the street. Never discovering how or where the women went in their immaculate saris, I copied Carol and walked confidently into hotels to use their more acceptable facilities.

India was full of contradictions and cultural conventions

that were difficult for me to understand. The nose-blowing made sense, but Indian men, young, old, militarily upright or raggedly rough, holding hands like primary school children on an outing was puzzling to this Westerner. I was used to such displays of affection by heterosexual couples, but here it was denied to young lovers and married couples alike.

I also found it difficult to understand why uncovered limbs were unacceptable but bare, wobbly midriffs between sari folds were OK. I'd noticed that it was often older women of assorted European nationalities who, oblivious or indifferent to local dress conventions, wandered the streets in shorts and skimpy T-shirts a size or two smaller than their thighs and chests merited.

I don't know if it was my imagination but the stares these women received seemed to have a contemptuous edge. The young backpackers, faithful followers of Rough Guide or Lonely Planet advice, were usually covered, and the looks given to these tanned youngsters appeared to lack that disdain. I wondered if the locals appreciated the Western women who tried not to offend, or whether we were all lumped together as loose and provocative.

The relentless pace of the tour continued as we left Rajasthan to drive north to the big, busy city of Agra. Here we parted company with Manesh, who'd steered us unscathed along hundreds of miles of crazy roads, avoiding pigs, broken-down lorries marked off with big stone boulders, manic scooters and immovable cows, his pose, poise and hair gel never once faltering. He had obviously decided to take on the strong, silent role, as it was difficult to get any conversation out of him despite his excellent English.

∞

At 6am the next morning we walked through a park to the Taj Mahal. Would the Taj, one of the world's most photographed buildings, live up to the promise, the hype and the 1,000 rupee (£6) entrance fee? Part of the mystique comes from the romance of the story of Shah Jahan taking ten years to build a marble mausoleum in memory of his favourite wife, who died giving birth to their seventeenth child.

Once inside the grounds, a reverential hush prevailed among the visitors waiting in the early morning mist. It was an unnerving quiet with something missing; only gradually did I realise that it was the unrelenting, noisy hubbub of India that was absent. There were no tugs at my sleeve from emaciated beggars or children with missing limbs, no women thrusting babies at me, no boys asking where I was from and no one trying to bless me – only an expectant silence.

As the sun forced its way above the horizon and over the thick layer of grey pollution, a low whisper began to emanate from the crowd, rising to a murmur as, at last, the sunlight broke through. Suddenly the Taj came into sharp focus, the pink tinge of the dawn light imbuing it with a fairy-tale glow against the brightness of the new day's blue sky. It was smaller than I expected, with that pristine neatness of a replica in a model village, and perfectly symmetrical, with its inlaid arches and graceful dome framed by the four identical minarets. I had expected to be impressed but the emotion it evoked came as a surprise. The exquisite grace and beauty of the building somehow encapsulated the love that inspired its creation and my heart responded.

The perfect mirror image shimmered on the water of the lake, the Celestial Pool of Abundance. Content to wait until the view was relatively clear of Japanese holding up two fingers, families of small Indians and groups of large Germans, I captured my shot of the Taj and its reflection. In contrast to the vivid whiteness of the exterior, a soft dappled light shone inside through the pierced marble of the windows and the screen round the two cenotaphs of Shah Jahan and his wife, breaking up the geometric precision of the symmetrical arches and colonnades and creating little sparkles as it caressed the inlaid jewels.

Not able to sustain reverence for long, I wandered around the formal rectangular gardens with their refreshing water channels. I couldn't resist a photo of Bruce sitting on the seat where Lady Diana posed, forlorn eyes looking up from bowed head, after her marriage was revealed to be in trouble.

In the evening we prepared to catch the sleeper train to our last destination in India, Varanasi. The station pulsed with the usual collection of destitute flotsam, swelled by the many pilgrims heading for the sacred city on the banks of the Ganges, one of the holiest spots on earth to both Hindus and Muslims. A travel rep met us with our tickets and waited like an athlete on the starting blocks to claim our berths once the train arrived.

Standing beside us was a young backpacker clutching his ticket, continuously jiggling as if he wanted the toilet and quite obviously terrified. He was a reminder that soon I would be on my own and I wondered how many situations comparable to an Indian train journey lay ahead. Would I cope? An idea was born.

'Carol,' I asked in my most persuasive voice, 'how do you fancy being my personal guide for the next five months?'

'And what's in it for me?' asked Carol, ever practical.

'Well, I couldn't pay you but I would guarantee a mention every week in my report.'

'Mmm, much as I might appreciate being a web star, I think I'll stick with tour-leading. Small pay is better than no pay.'

'Oh well, alone it is,' I sighed.

The train arrived and, as our agent parted the crowd to get us aboard, I glimpsed the young man running up and down the platform trying to locate his berth. I never saw him again.

We had a small cramped cabin to ourselves with a curtain dividing us from the three layered berths along the other side of the carriage. After chaining our bags to immovable fixtures, we tried our best to sleep through the hot, airless but uneventful night.

∞

Varanasi was a maze of lanes, too narrow even for rickshaws, with little shrines in every niche and doorway. Untidy layers

39

of temples, flats, monasteries and shrines were stacked up the banks of the Ganges, a river so wide that the far side was hidden by the inevitable layer of pollution. The sadhus here were very different from the pretend ones who besieged the tourists in the rest of India; they walked with a dignity and a sense of purpose, ignoring the tourists.

The next day saw another pre-dawn rising to catch our boat on the Ganges. Although it was still dark, the ghats were crowded with devotees here to bathe or to die, and the widowed and elderly who sought shelter in the temples on the riverbank to live out what might otherwise be destitute days. A priest was chanting prayers and twirling small braziers on chains. We floated past the cremation areas where the sad but dignified work continues day and night, sending those cremated at Varanasi to instant moksha – freedom from the endless cycle of birth, death and rebirth. Two ceremonies were about to begin; a red shroud denoting a woman and yellow a man, and little candles were lit and set afloat on the river, twinkling as dawn rose.

Varanasi felt like a special place, even to an atheist like me. I could almost touch the air of devotion, feel the intensity of the prayers and sense the effect of the holy water on the bathers, for many of whom this was a once-in-a-lifetime pilgrimage. Women in saris with babies, portly middle-aged men, skinny youths and skeletal old men soaped, prayed, dunked and soaked in the soupy grey water.

I'm normally sceptical and the presence of religious faith, be it shiny-eyed Christians singing, Jews wailing at the wall or Islamic students rocking while reading the Koran, sends shivers of unease down my spine. Here, the bathers awakened a tiny dormant part of me that envied those who have the security and certainty of a faith. I discarded religion at the age of thirteen, much to my mother's dismay. She had prayed for me every day but her god evidently had better things to do than send a thunderbolt of either revelation or retribution onto this sinner, as I remain unscathed and unsaved.

Nevertheless, I've not been able to escape my birthright:

guilt. Nobody appeared to mind the boats full of tourists but I felt uncomfortable in this holiest of places and questioned what I was doing here. Was I an interested, sympathetic spectator bringing my spending power to a poor people, or merely a voyeur exploiting those less fortunate in my thirst for new experiences? I couldn't answer.

∞

The next day was our last in India, as we were catching the bus for Nepal. For days Carol had been preparing us for the discomfort of this journey but hitherto all her warnings of 'simple' hotels or 'humble' restaurants had proved groundless as we had crossed marble thresholds to go up sweeping staircases and eaten sublime food. The bus station was a hut with a tiny fire for cooking and a wooden bench to sit on where we were given an omelette sandwich and a cup of chai. The passengers were backpackers of assorted nationalities and we were adopted by a Brummie of the been-there-done-that variety.

'Hi, how've you been getting on in India? Oi think it's great – Oi've only spent a few quid and Oi've been here months.'

When we showed little interest in his ability to live off the land and its people, he moved on to a young French couple.

'Oi'd been doing really well not spending any money until Oi met this carpet-seller who slipped something into my drink. Oi thought Oi was a gonner.'

'Oooh, mon dieu,' exclaimed the horrified mademoiselle.

Emboldened, he droned on with tales of nearly getting robbed, nearly getting drugged, nearly getting laid – and nearly all for free...

Eventually our transport arrived, a ramshackle antique bus with more rust than solid metal. We watched our precious bags being thrown on top, praying that the roof and the rope would support them. Carol and I were moved from the front seat because a boy had to sit there to scream at passing taxis while he held the piece of string that kept the door shut.

We watched the driver trying to find a place for his flip-flopped feet amongst the tangle of wires hanging down from the steering wheel. Resplendent in traditional white baggy trousers and colourful embroidered top, he was the spitting image of Omar Sharif, but disillusionment set in when he smiled to reveal a mouthful of teeth stained bright red by pann (betel nut), a mild narcotic. At first I'd wondered what the red blobs all over the streets were – blood, paint or religious markings? They were, in fact, discarded globules of red juice produced by pann. Walking the streets of India, you had to be nimble to dodge the streams of cow and human urine and betel juice.

Many hours of shaking, bouncing and rattling through north India left my body feeling as though it had been attached to a pneumatic drill. In the absence of catches, the sliding windows whipped back and forth, somehow staying in their frames, and the lack of suspension made Claire and Mike very sick. Occasional 'comfort' stops were taken at the roadside, where everyone rushed to claim a bush, the more fastidious searching deep into the trees for an unsullied spot. I ventured so far that, but for Carol, the bus would have left without me.

All discomfort was forgotten when, on a sharp bend, we scraped an oncoming jeep, leaving a trail of wheel arch and fibreglass behind. Ten beefy men piled out of the jeep, limping and rubbing their heads as they bore down on the bus. Omar stayed resolutely in his seat as the shouting and arm-waving began. All hope of using the opportunity to find a clean bush disappeared as a crowd of curious little boys gathered to watch the fun. After a couple of hours, the vocal cords and the arms grew tired and the situation was resolved – I've no idea how – and we drove off, only to stop ten minutes later at a garage to have our brakes mended.

At 9pm we finally reached the border crossing, which housed a collection of scruffy hostels and money-changing booths. The first job was to go to the checkpoint to get our stamp to enter Nepal. For the less organised who hadn't secured a visa in advance, obtaining one involved an additional $50. There was a handsome Frenchman behind me in the queue who asked to borrow $50 as his money was in Swiss francs. Seeing my dubious expression, he gave me a big bundle of francs to keep as security, so I agreed.

I'd noticed him on the bus, not only because he was rugged and lean, but also because he kept himself very much to himself. Sneaking a look at his passport full of stamps in and out of India and Nepal, I decided he must be a spy or smuggler and wondered, if he were caught, if I would be arrested for aiding and abetting. The one attraction of this scenario would be if we shared a cell. He appeared later with $50 and counted it out note by note. 'Ten, twenty, thirty, forty, fifty.'

He delivered each number with that erotic sensuousness unique to the French, and I was tempted to insist on single dollar notes to prolong the pleasure. Instead I was reduced to a tongue-tied teenager and just mumbled, 'Thank you.'

'Mon dieu,' moaned Carol. 'Please call him back to count it all over again.'

None of us bothered to wash or change at bedtime but flung our jaded bodies onto the hostel's dirty beds. This was my last night in India but I couldn't work out how I felt about it. I knew I'd have struggled to cope with this vast, disorganised country on my own, as even on a tour it had been an exhausting experience, packed with delights, frustrations, wonders and horrors.

One image stuck in my mind: a glimpse as we drove past of two tiny children in immaculate bright blue blazers waiting for the school bus. They stood hand in hand on a derelict corner, ankle-deep in filth – a picture of both hope and despair.

3

A Trek Too Far

The next evening I was in Nepal, top of my travel wish list. In distant student years, I'd watched enviously as hippies took off in battered VW vans to wander Asia, but at that time I had neither the courage nor cash to join them. Thirty years later, here I was realising the dream, and I had to pinch myself to make sure it was real.

Surrounded by good companions, full of pasta and tiramisu and next to a roaring brazier, I was overcome by an intense feeling of happiness. Could life get much better than this? No worries, no work – just pure pleasure, every day brimming with new experiences. I felt giddy with elation, no doubt augmented by the third glass of house red, the first wine I'd drunk since leaving home.

In the morning, in a scruffy hostel on the Indian border, our departure was delayed by a near-riot on the bus, precipitated by two Israeli backpackers refusing to give the Indian boys the ten-rupee tip for loading their bags. It was a gladiatorial contest, the skinny porters in grubby white shifts facing down two big strapping youths in designer travel gear. The partisan audience booed and hissed in collective impatience and embarrassment until the lads were finally shamed into grudgingly handing over the equivalent of a few pence, and we were able to set off.

From the flat plains of India, we crossed the lowlands of Nepal and began to climb upwards towards the mountains.

In a much better quality bus than the previous day's, we chugged around and over steep forested hills. We passed through ramshackle villages of wooden houses where the villagers, often clustered around the busy communal tap washing themselves, their children, blackened pots or laundry, smiled and waved as we passed. If we slowed to pass a cow, a fruit barrow or triple-parked rickshaws, trays of oranges, flat bread and knick-knacks appeared out of nowhere to be thrust against the bus windows.

At the dilapidated bus station on the edge of Kathmandu, a local travel agent and his assistant escorted us to a waiting taxi. However, the local madman had got there first and was ensconced in the front passenger seat, mumbling contentedly into his matted beard. The agent, assistant and driver stood scratching their heads, reluctant to act until Carol took charge and bullied them into forcibly removing him. Next came the challenge of fitting the four of us (not forgetting that Mike was really one-and-a-half), agent, assistant and driver into one moderately sized car. I ended up with the agent on my knee, the closest I'd been to a man for a while.

Locals and tourists, touts selling Gurkha knives, cycle wallahs on their gaudy rickshaws and assorted shoe-shine boys formed a swirling, fast-moving river along Kathmandu's narrow streets. Within minutes I could have bought enough tiger balm to rival Body Shop, had my sandals polished till they shone and still had change for a few tin cups. Between the lines of little shops and stalls, bright banners and bunting criss-crossed the road, their colours competing with pashmina scarves, hand-woven carpets and traditional Buddhist paintings; these, in turn, vied with the inevitable selection of tie-dyed hippie clothes. Narrow alleys led to courtyard cafés and rickety stairs led to rooftop restaurants where the bright sunshades of the day were replaced by wood-burning braziers in the chilly evening. It was a blatant, garish assault upon the senses, and I loved it.

∞

The Kathmandu valley, packed with temple and palace complexes that reflected the assorted religions and dynasties of Nepal that had survived centuries of earthquakes and feuds, was as exciting and exotic as the capital. In Bodhnath, the all-seeing eye of Buddha painted on each side of the huge white stupa appeared to watch protectively over Tibetan exiles waiting to return to their own land. At Pashupatinath, housing Nepal's most important Hindu temple, devoted to the god Shiva, cremations were underway on the banks of the sacred Bagmati River.

But it was in Bhaktapur, once the capital of the valley, that I felt the full force of Nepal's history and beauty. To walk through the archway in the ancient city walls was to be transported to a more leisurely, aesthetic age. The Golden Gate, entrance to the fifty-five Window Palace, set the tone; the terracotta stone building was roofed in gold and covered in rich, elaborate carvings of multi-headed, multi-limbed gods disposing of their enemies.

Inside Durbar Square, architecture unlike any I'd seen before spread before me in a geometric maze. Square temples with single-pagoda roofs squatted beside those with tapering spires or five-terraced pagodas, supported by elaborately carved wooden struts. Every temple stood on a stone plinth, often as high as the temple itself, the stairways adorned with carved animals and gods. Giant bronze bells, terracotta palaces and statues of kings, elephants, lions and gods in both benign and terrible manifestations, lined the square.

A short walk led to another square, the Taumadhi Tole, where Nepal's tallest building, a five-storey pagoda called the Nyatapola Temple, soared imperiously into the cloudless azure sky. Looking at the steps guarded by two famous wrestlers, two elephants, two lions, two griffins and Baghini and Singhini (the tiger and lion goddesses), each rising in their power of protection by the factor of ten, I wondered if today's architects would be humble enough to place man at the bottom.

In the narrow lanes between the squares, the townsfolk were going about their business: women were drying grain on the ground; dyed yarn hung on long washing lines; piles of pots and pans, baskets overflowing with fruit, vegetables and spices stood for sale, and local artists worked in little galleries. I walked slowly, enjoying the calm timelessness and smiling in anticipation of what might be round the next corner. In yet another square, potters worked on wheels in the open, teasing the lumps of stubborn clay into smooth, graceful shapes until they were ready to join the regimented ranks of utilitarian pots and jugs, arty artisan vases and touristy elephants baking in the hot sun.

The sound of cymbals heralded a procession led by men and boys carrying red flags, banners and beating barrel-shaped drums. I asked a shopkeeper what it was. 'Festival of Vishnu – to thank the god for making the days longer and warmer as winter passes.'

Following the men were women and pretty, smiling girls in beautiful, bright saris trimmed with gold, forming a patchwork to rival Joseph's coat. The setting of Bhaktapur, the simplicity of the procession, the clothes and instruments, made me feel I was witnessing life as it would have been in medieval times. The only incongruity was me and my digital camera.

∞

Nepal was living up to all my expectations but I still hadn't seen the mountains; so, on the last free day of the tour, I headed out to Nagarkot for my first glimpse of the Himalayas. The taxi, spluttering and wheezing, stuttered its way up the narrow, twisting road, the engine in tune with the grumbles of the driver as he paid at the village checkpoints. Our destination was a hilltop hotel and, leaving the car and driver to their mutual misery, I rushed up a path to the large patio that looked out to the Himalayas. Gazing towards the ragged, sharp peaks that stretched along the horizon like the monitor of an irregular heartbeat, my spirits rose. I wondered yet again why I lived in East Anglia, with its bleak, flat landscape of treeless, sunken black earth.

My quiet contemplation was disturbed by a rumble coming from the steep slope behind me; as it grew in volume I turned, curious to see what was approaching. First over the brow of the hill was a medieval siege engine pushed by a small army of T-shirted soldiers carrying assorted weapons. A portly, sweating general followed, with a swarm of girls in sickly green saris bringing up the rear. As a camera was loaded onto a crane and order began to emerge from the tangle of wires and swirling green silk, it became apparent that this wasn't the Nagarkot Liberation Army but a production company here to make a music video.

Watching and listening to the producer shout in desperation, it was obvious that these dancers were not from Nepal's elite dancing academies. The girls displayed a collective inability to move in unison, bumping into each other constantly, one even tripping over to form a green puddle. A hyperactive assistant raced around them like a sheepdog on speed, wielding his clapper board with aggressive bravado.

Snap, music, bump, groan, snap – the ritual was repeated, again and again, until the inept dancers had been cowed into some semblance of rhythmic harmony. At that point the singer, who had been lounging nearby adjusting the angle of his white Panama hat, deigned to join in. He had a pleasant voice, with that Bollywood ability to sing what sounded like a sad song with a cheeky grin and jaunty energy.

When they took a break to rest the producer's throat and the clapper boy's arms, I struck a deal: a photo for the website in exchange for a plug of the record. Dutifully the singer and dancers posed with the Himalayas as backdrop and I mentioned Sunil Lama's new disc, called Bhinte Bishauchha, in my next report.

Over the following weeks I received no word of a rush to HMV, and scouring Kathmandu's record shops to find anything by my friend Sunil drew a total blank. His business card had an address in Germany. Was the record a front for nefarious activities connected to the handsome French smuggler I aided and abetted on the Nepalese border?

As the tour wound up I wound down, not aware until then just how tired I was after the frenetic activity of the preceding weeks. Kathmandu, with no tight tour schedule, an abundance of rooftop cafés, plenty of alternatives to curry and friendly, laid-back people, was the perfect place to relax.

Sitting with a beer in the bright sun, looking down on the busy street below, I remembered with a start that it was Christmas Eve, a strange thought in a land so far away in culture and miles. How different it would be at home: cold, probably wet and busy with stressed last-minute Christmas shoppers trying to find substitutes for the unavailable CD/toy/ perfume requested by their loved ones. A few shop windows had little plastic Christmas trees and tinsel for the tourists but they were inconsequential among the everyday colour of Kathmandu.

This would be my first Christmas away from home but at least it saved all the post-divorce angst about 'turns' and reconstituted families that transformed Christmas into a strategic nightmare.

I've never been a great fan of Christmas. Even when the children were small, I was dismayed by the mountain of presents under the tree – garish plastic toys, novelty gifts of chocolate golf balls, burping bottle-openers and Winnie-the-Pooh socks, straight-off-to-Oxfam table mats, woollen gloves and stinky soap. I should have started travelling years before.

The evening was spent in Kathmandu's 'Irish bar', where we squeezed in among the young backpackers and Nepalese men. In honour of the dubious ethnicity of the bar, I was going to order a Guinness.

'Don't touch it, mate,' said a young Australian propping up the bar next to me, 'unless you want to spend Christmas in the dunnie.'

I looked blank.

'It'll give you the shits,' he explained.

'Thanks,' I said, and ordered a bottled beer.

'No worries.'

A local band, clearly feeling the evening chill in anoraks and woolly hats, was playing a mixture of Dire Straits, Bob Marley and Nepalese pop songs. The audience was sedentary until the band struck the first notes of a local tune whereupon, as if stabbed by a cattle prod, every Nepalese man leapt to his feet and launched into strange, hip-swivelling, arm-waving gyrations. The moment the band reverted to Western music, they took their seats again.

With this surreal game of musical 'Simon Says' in the background Mike, who had a built-in time-zone clock, tracked Santa as he deposited his load.

'I reckon he's crossing New Zealand now,' said Mike, with a nostalgic or drunken tear in his eye. And so it continued over Japan and China before Mike proclaimed, on the stroke of midnight, that he had reached Kathmandu. We toasted the moment with our beers and I staggered off to bed.

∞

As I woke up on Christmas morning in Kathmandu, with the bright sun chasing away the chill of the night, the only harbinger of Christmas was the card that thoughtful ex-boyfriend Philip had put in my luggage.

'Happy Christmas, Bruce,' I said to break the unnatural silence of this festive morning. I'd left behind little presents for my children, so at least they would think of me when opening them. I waited until they would be at their father's for Christmas dinner to make my first phone call home.

'Hello it's–'
'...Is that...'
'...me.'
'...Mum? It's Ben.'
'Happy Christmas!'
'Where are you?'
'I'm in–'
'Hi Mum, it's...'
'Kathmandu.'

'Sam now.'

'I miss you.'

'...it's Rachel. We miss...'

'Love—'

'...you, mum.'

That was it, over, leaving me feeling angry, deflated and cheated by a line so abysmal and with a time delay so confusing that I had no idea which child I was talking to. It reminded me of the first post-divorce Christmas Day, when I dropped the children off at a full ex-in-law gathering and, feeling sad and excluded, returned home alone to shed a few tears. For the first time, homesickness swept over me and I ached to hug my children so much that I was tempted to jump on the first plane to England. But it was a transitory moment.

It was a consolation to have Christmas dinner with a group, swollen to nine with Carol's new tour and a couple of stray Brits. I've never had pasta for Christmas dinner before but it was a minor first among so many. Carol had made everyone Christmas crackers with a sweet inside but she hadn't been able to find the snappers for the middle so we all had to shout 'bang!' as we pulled them.

After dinner it was time to say an emotional goodbye to Claire and Mike, who were flying back to New Zealand early in the morning after three years' absence. I would miss sharing dawns, vicariously enduring their tummy troubles, jumping out of the path of the airborne Rough Guide to India (a very large tome) as they argued over which way to go round a palace, making myself scarce when they made up – oh, happy days. They promised to follow my adventures on the net, and I vowed to look them up when I reached Wellington.

∞

It felt OK for the tour to end in Kathmandu as I felt comfortable there and, after three weeks, I'd lost my initial terror of Asia. However, my complacency was short-lived as on Boxing Day afternoon I walked out of my hotel straight into a three-deep phalanx of riot police with machine guns, large batons and riot shields. What was going on? Everything felt and sounded wrong, with the clamouring vendors, the bells of the cycle wallahs and the noisy crowds laughing, hawking and spitting replaced by distant muffled bangs and the sharp clanking of metal shutters as shopkeepers hurriedly closed their shops.

This wasn't supposed to happen to a novice backpacker on her first day alone. Confused and cowardly, I retreated back into the hotel to sit out on the veranda. The only other occupant was a shaven-headed young man whose body language hinted at Hannibal Lector appetites. I'd noticed him before, either exercising dementedly or lying comatose plugged into a Walkman. I'd never heard him speak or seen him leave the balcony.

An excited young German rushed through the courtyard below shouting, 'Rioting, teargas in the streets!'

The skinhead shot to his feet and roared out a torrent of Franglais expletives: 'Fucking Commies! Bastards! Fucking tout le monde!'

When he began pacing up and down, eyes blazing, fists clenched, I was afraid that he might have a secret radar that could tune into the faintest of left-wing tendencies, so I retreated to my room.

I took a nap in the hope that the afternoon could be written off as a bad dream and that I could laugh about it with Carol's new tour when I met them in the evening to go to a dance show. Apprehensively, I left the safety of my hotel, avoiding the balcony, to scurry the few hundred yards to our meeting point. Stepping into gloomy darkness, there was no neon from shops and bars, no kerosene lamps hanging from stalls, nor even an occasional car headlight. The rows of dull metal shutters turned the street into an eerie alley full of dangerous doorways, with the bunting overhead flapping menacingly like large bats black against the dark grey sky. The absence of the usual crowds and noise was alarming, and I clutched Bruce for comfort.

'Oh Bruce, I want to be pestered by dope sellers and shoeshine boys. Where are the cycle wallahs when you really want one?'

I quickened my step, keeping to the centre of the road and avoiding eye contact with any of the shadowy forms that hurried by. The only stationary figures were the guards standing stoically at each hotel entrance, hands hovering near holsters. The one outside my destination decided that a tourist clutching a little teddy bear was no danger to the safety of his establishment and opened the door just enough for me to squeeze through into the bright foyer.

I met the three new Imaginative Travellers in the lobby, but they were no wiser about what was happening. It took the guard and two hotel staff setting off in different directions to find a taxi prepared to take us to the other side of town at an extortionate price. We were so late that we were convinced the show would be almost over, but the proprietor met us at the door

'Welcome, welcome, so pleased you come.'

'So sorry we're late. Have we missed most of the show?' I said as we hastened inside.

'No, no worries. We wait for you.'

We were flattered until we realised that we were the entire audience and the colourful display of traditional dancing and music began the moment we sat down. Dishes of nibbles were provided and small bowls of a very fiery liquid that I alone liked so, finding that it had a marked effect of easing the tension of my evening expedition, I drank all four bowls. Being quite shy and having little sense of rhythm, it still remains a mystery how I found myself on stage jigging self-consciously beside a dancer dressed as a yeti in a suit of mop-heads. Someone grabbed my camera and the moment was captured.

A few days later in a very high-tech internet café I came across an intriguing email from the Guardian, which said, 'Loved the yeti film, it made my day.' What was that about? The assistant helped me open the link and the awful truth was revealed. There wasn't a picture of me and my hairy friend but a five-second movie of us 'dancing'. The assistant's spectacles fell off as he roared with laughter and shouted in Nepalese to the other earnest young men crouched over their keyboards. Soon I was surrounded by a crowd of chuckling youths who leaned over to press the repeat button every time I tried to move on, while silently begging my children's forgiveness for any embarrassment they might suffer.

After the show the streets were deserted and gloomy, but the promise of another large sum persuaded our taxi driver to return us to our respective hotels. I had to pass on my goodbyes to Carol, sad that I couldn't see her before the group left for India early next morning.

∞

Now I was truly in a new phase of my trip, travelling alone and without Carol as Pied Piper to lead me to wonderful sights, delicious food and wholesome accommodation. Thank heavens for Rough Guides and Lonely Planets; they were inferior but adequate substitutes.

There was no way I could have foreseen being marooned in a city and crawling with police and army. Hunger got the better of fear but, as I crossed the hotel threshold, I ran straight into a hundred or so grim-faced, black-clothed young men marching and chanting in unison, waving the Nepalese and other political flags. It was a far cry from the good-humoured, boisterous student rallies of my youth. Police and army stood on every street corner but let the procession pass unhindered.

In my usual breakfast café, a couple from Yorkshire with access to a TV told me the cause of all this trouble. Any number of possibilities had crossed my mind, from royal indiscretion, political or marital adultery, or even a new tax on shoe polish, but I would never have thought of an Indian Bollywood star. Hrithik Roshan, India's Brad Pitt, was alleged to have said on a TV chat show that he hated Nepal and its people, whereupon the Nepalese, understandably affronted, burned down an Indian cinema in Kathmandu showing Hrithik's latest blockbuster. Despite Mr Roshan's vigorous denials, and suspicions that it was all a rumour started by the Indian mafia miffed that they didn't get the distribution rights to Roshan's film, the situation degenerated into widespread political unrest and culminated in a national strike, with roadblocks appearing all round Kathmandu. I thought it lucky that the French, Irish, Americans and Germans aren't so sensitive, or British comedians would create international mayhem.

It was difficult to comprehend the change in both atmosphere and activity in Kathmandu. The streets were empty of all but a few backpackers wandering aimlessly. Although there didn't appear to be any threat to tourists, there also wasn't much to do, as only a few brave souls had kept food and internet cafés open.

One consequence of the strike, minor in the grand scale of things but worrying to someone with so few clothes, was that there was no sign of my laundry, which would soon precipitate a knicker crisis. More urgent than clean underwear was the need for bottled water; it was only on reaching the edge of the tourist area of Thamel that I found a shop with its shutter open about a foot. On bended knees I shouted and waved through the gap until a disembodied arm appeared with a bottle of water, snatched the money and withdrew into its sanctuary.

I've never had a very good sense of direction; on my way back I took a wrong turning and found my way barred by an acrid-smelling pile of burning tyres. The roadblock was manned by a large band of agitated men studying a poster pinned to a telegraph pole, luckily too preoccupied to notice a trembling middle-aged woman clutching a bottle of water. Although I couldn't understand the words, I could pick up the anger and passion in their voices and tried not to run as I hurriedly retraced my steps back to the comparative safety of the main street.

The tour's end had led not only to the departure of my companions and Kathmandu's descent into chaos, but also to the move into backpacker accommodation. After one very damp night in the Kathmandu Guesthouse, where my towel was wetter in the morning than after the shower the day before, I booked into The Star. It was a scruffy, rambling collection of rooms but very cheap and, as I was to discover, with very thin walls.

Each night I entered a nightmare tower of Babel offering stereophonic language classes all on the same subject: sex. I was to learn that backpackers are a very lusty lot.

On the left was a guttural Scandinavian tongue: 'Oh ja, oh ja, JAAAAAAA!' That Norwegian must have been faking it.

Later, more romantic Gallic sounds breached the thin wall: 'Oooooo, encore, mais oui.' At least this was an established couple so it shouldn't take long.

Just when I thought it was all over and I could get to sleep, squeaky Far Eastern started behind me: 'Eeeek, yeee, eeeeeeyo.' They'd only just met and would be at it for hours.

The end of the strike came just before insomnia, envy and madness overwhelmed me. As soon as Kathmandu, and Nepal, returned to its normal noisy self, I left the city for the mountains.

∞

The next morning I was up at dawn to catch the bus to Pokhara, which sits at the bottom of the Annapurna mountain range. I felt nervous leaving the familiarity of Kathmandu but excited at the prospect of my first solo excursion.

Seven hours later, after passing through cultivated valleys alongside a wide river, the bus driver dropped me in the middle of a town heaving with people, impromptu bars, shops and discos blasting out Western pop music. What had happened to the quiet, laid-back place of the guidebooks? I discovered that it wasn't riots or video shoots disturbing the peace this time but a two-day festival to celebrate the king's birthday.

Dotted along the main street were little village bands, women in matching embroidered traditional dresses and men in flamboyant breeches and billowing shirts, singing and dancing. Unfortunately the tinkling bells, acoustic guitars and pipes struggled to be heard above the deep throbbing beat of the disco vans.

One group of dancers wore large elaborate masks depicting

spirits and monsters. Their leader consented enthusiastically when I asked if I could take a picture, but the men themselves became quite distressed when asked to pose, believing perhaps the flash would have the same effect as my mother's warning when I was pulling a face: 'You'll stay like that if the wind changes…' This was the first time I'd seen any fear of the camera and, dismayed to be caught in the middle of a battle of wills between the dancers and their leader, I sloped off to have a look round Pokhara.

The town is built on the edge of the large, serene Lake Phewa, set against a backdrop of mountains, but a grey mist obscured all but the lower dark slopes, matching my gloomy mood as I wandered through the festive streets. Food and internet often lifted my spirits, so I sought both.

There were cafés and restaurants serving European food dotted around the lake but I spurned these in favour of one full of Nepalese so I could try the staple Nepal dish, dal bhat. A plate containing a mound of rice, a clump of vegetables, a dollop of lentils and some unidentifiable meat arrived. I watched the locals mix all this up and scoop it into their mouths with their hands, but I accepted the offered fork gratefully. It took but a few mouthfuls to realise I'd made a grave mistake: the meat was solid gristle, the rice was stodgy and the sauce was bitter.

Neither did I have much luck with the internet, which was very slow and seven times the price of that in Kathmandu. Would I end up judging the places I visited by the quality of their internet facilities? Those in India had been slow and erratic, often failing as I was about to press the send button after spending an hour loading my photographs. Kathmandu's had been excellent and in the riot days I'd been able to catch up on the Netjetter emails sent by readers, a mixture of recommendations and good wishes. There wasn't much else to do that day but go to bed and try to sleep through the disco music.

∞

The next day was New Year's Eve, another misty day spent wandering the streets alone. I wasn't getting on well with Pokhara and didn't see the reputed scenery owing to the cloud which, in the afternoon, turned to rain, the first I'd seen for a month.

That evening, finding the last free table at a steak house, I ate my solitary steak and drank my solitary beer, feeling very lonely and sad. The tour was a good start and I loved Kathmandu, but after nearly a week without conversation and now in a strange town full of partygoers, I was feeling sorry for myself. By 10pm, having run out of things to do, I went to bed, tossing and turning as I suffered my first 'what am I doing here?' moments. At 3am the discos shut down and I slept.

∞

I woke up on a new day in a new year, bleary-eyed but with a change of mood. The blues of the preceding day were banished by excitement as I was about to embark on my first-ever mountain trek. The plan drawn up by the hotel manager entailed meeting my guide here at 7am, taking a taxi for 12kms, walking to Dhampus in the mountains, staying there overnight, walking to Sarangkot and taxiing back – a nice two-day expedition well within my capabilities. The Nepalese, however, had other plans, as the country was again gripped by a two-day strike and neither guide nor taxi turned up. The manager was unfazed.

'I take you but bad leg. No worry, I find you guide,' he said as he walked off with a previously unnoticeable limp. He was only gone a few minutes, returning with a diminutive figure dressed in jeans, a thin shirt and a large woolly hat.

Dubious as to my new guide's authenticity, I fired off questions. 'How old is he?'

'Seventeen.'

'Has he done any trekking?'

'Oh yes.'

'Does he speak English?'

58

'A little.'

'How are we to get to the mountains?'

'Walk.'

I peered under the woolly hat and asked the lad his name. 'Rajis,' he muttered shyly as he stuffed a jacket into a rucksack.

The choice was go along with this or lose half my money and hang around Pokhara for the next few days – no choice, really. Rajis squeezed my sleeping bag into his rucksack, I shouldered my own bag and we set off. As we walked out of Pokhara and along the empty roads, any hope of a passing taxi or lift evaporated. Conversation was very limited as Rajis could understand only basic English, but he had a very sweet smile and would often break into the latest Nepalese hit song, thankfully without the gyrations.

After three hours my hips, calves and feet were aching and I gesticulated to Rajis that I needed a sit-down and breakfast. In the next village he found a tiny roadside café and the woman in charge sent off one of her barefooted children in search of bread, leaving the other four to stare at me with big, round brown eyes. Eventually they tired and returned to their skipping game and after an egg inside a stale roll and two tin cups of the Nepalese version of chai, the protesting legs were set in motion again.

The valley stretched ahead endlessly but at least the mountains could now be glimpsed through the low cloud. I made Rajis stop a couple of times so I could rest, watching the women hoeing in the fields.

A couple of hours later we stopped for lunch at a bench outside a house, where the menu was dal bhat with or without meat, instantly re-converting me to vegetarianism. The lady-of-the-bench bustled busily, dividing herself between cooking our food, changing a baby's nappy and shooing the chickens off the table. Rajis tucked into his meal with gusto and hand, while I picked at mine with the fork she'd managed to find. I don't think my dal bhat was strictly vegetarian, as I'm sure it was laced with chicken and baby poo. After eating a little, I tried hard to convince myself that I didn't need a pee but had to ask to use the bathroom, a shed with a plank over a malodorous hole in the ground.

After lunch we walked for another half hour until a near-vertical mountainside appeared straight ahead. Rajis looked innocently pleased with himself as he said, 'We go up here.' An old man sitting at the base of the monster hill registered the foreboding on my face and produced a long staff out of nowhere for me to buy.

For three tough hours we climbed the rough rock steps, punctuated every few minutes by my compulsion to stop and pant furiously for breath. (Yet another vow was taken to give up smoking.) Not only did my calf muscles scream in protest but I also strained a groin muscle, which made each lift of the foot very painful. Bruce, out of my bag for periodic photo shoots, had to endure my pain.

'Twenty more steps, Bruce, and then I will kill Rajis so we can go home.'

'Thirty steps to that boulder, Bruce, where I suspect that I'm going to expire.'

'I hate mountains – why do they have to be so bloody high?'

At every bend I prayed that the top would be round the next corner but each one revealed yet more steps winding ever upward. Occasionally, during the frequent rests, I summoned enough energy to take in the view of the valley below and consoled myself that anyone would be tired after walking its length.

At one point, a Nepalese man out for a stroll joined us and quizzed me about life in the UK.

'You put your old people in special homes, I believe,' he said in excellent English. I tried to explain that there were a variety of options but he interrupted by asking, 'Do you live in one of these homes?' Obviously I looked as bad as I felt.

As dusk fell, I was so tired that it wasn't until we were actually walking into Dhampus, a small village perched 1,750 metres high on the edge of the mountain, that I realised the steps had ended. In one of the string of lodges along the road, we were taken along a wooden veranda to a room containing three beds. As I collapsed on the nearest one, Rajis cast me an anxious look to see if I was going to challenge the room-sharing, but I was too tired to care and suspected that if I'd objected, he would have had to sleep on the floor somewhere. After an hour, not sure if the numbness was due to cold or rigor mortis, I forced myself to get up and join Rajis in the open-air porch that doubled as restaurant.

Soon it was far too cold to be outside and I asked to sit by the fire in the kitchen where the mother fed the baby, the children chased an exhausted puppy and their father presided benignly over the scene. I felt I was watching an old movie depicting idyllic rural life and, on cue, an aged grandma in a colourful shawl and thick woollen skirt arrived, did a little dance for my benefit and then left.

The family appeared very happy, amusing itself without TV, computer or any mod-con at all but when I found myself envying their simple life and simple pleasure, I felt both hypocritical and guilty. I only had to spend one night here, an extremely cold one, and had blanched at the very basic squat loo below our veranda, with only a tap outside for washing.

At 7pm, Rajis and I retired to bed. Pausing to give my teeth a cursory brush and remove my boots, I crawled into my sleeping bag under a thick quilt and immediately fell asleep. At midnight I woke up sweating and stumbled around to find torch, boots and coat, wondering if I was going to throw up over the sleeping Rajis. A dose of freezing fresh air on the way to the loo, a swig of water and I felt well enough to go back to bed, this time minus the heavy quilt.

∞

Rajis woke me at 7am with a cup of chai. How civilised, I thought: tea in bed. But Rajis kept demanding, 'Come look! Come look!' It took great willpower to leave my cosy sleeping bag and stumble out onto the veranda but what I saw amply compensated for the aching muscles and hardship of the day before. Straight ahead, framed by bright blue sky with only puffs of gauze-like cloud, were the snow-capped Annapurnas, the dark, pitted, craggy slopes leading up to brilliant white peaks illuminated by the sun. Highest in the range was Machhapuchhre, the Fishtail Mountain, so steep that the sharp-pointed peak was brown, barren rock, the snow sliding down crevasses like white veins.

When Rajis took me to a hill outside the village with more panoramic views, a group of four Korean students arrived, gabbling away excitedly as we took pictures of each other with the mountains as backdrop. Their more convincing guide took my fledgling Rajis under his wing and we teamed up for the return walk.

The next couple of hours were downhill and gradually we began to shed layers of clothing as the day and our muscles warmed up. I felt surprisingly well and it seemed easier walking in company, especially as one of the Korean girls – with a name that sounded as painful as her expression – was struggling more than me. I re-christened her Dumpling as she was plump and round and rolled from side to side, either exhaustion or Nepalese food preventing her from walking in a straight line. We often had to wait for her to weave her way back to the group, muttering and sighing to herself in Korean.

I was enjoying myself until we reached the bottom of the hill and another monster loomed in front of us. 'Yes, we go up there,' was the answer to my anxious question. As we rested, gathering our strength, an enterprising local arrived in his ancient car and offered to take us by road to the top for a hundred rupees each. Not wanting to appear a wimp, I waited for the Korean group's decision but couldn't disguise my glee when, on Dumpling's pleading, they decided to take the car. There was a little roadside café at the top and the breakfast of scrambled eggs with Tibetan bread invigorated me enough to walk again. The next few hours were undulating but not too steep, and just about manageable.

A joke developed that I was Rajis' mother and he would ask, 'Mommy OK?'

'No, I'm fine, my boy. Thank you, anyway.'

'Mommy tired; Rajis carry bag.'

I was actually beginning to feel quite maternal towards the lad.

We passed a group of Nepalese bearers, mostly women, trudging along with enormous baskets tied to their heads with leather headbands, each containing the tents and backpacks of tourist trekkers. The size and weight of those baskets brought back my unease about the impact of tourism; although I knew that this is their living and they may not have one without this trade, it looked like such hard work. I was struggling with only my little rucksack.

When we approached small settlements, the children all rushed towards us, thrusting out grubby hands, clamouring:

'Pens pliz.'

'Sweets pliz.'

'Money pliz.'

I walked along chanting, 'No sweets, no pens, no money,' at the top of my voice, and as I sang and laughed they laughed with me – no hard feelings on either side.

At the rest stops along the way, the Koreans shared their snacks. I had to discreetly spit out the stick of dried fish that tasted like week-old chip paper, although the strips of seaweed were very tasty. I didn't have much to share, only a few battered sweets, but Phil, one of the Koreans, was curious about my roll-ups. The vow to give up for the trip had been modified to only a few roll-ups a day, in the delusional belief that I would smoke less. Many Asians had watched wide-eyed at the sight of a middle-aged woman spreading a few miserly clumps of tobacco along a piece of paper, licking it, cussing as it fell apart, trying again and finally setting fire to the skinny, limp, saliva-stained excuse for a cigarette.

'I try, pleez,' asked Phil, and I passed him one of my better efforts. He took one puff, pulled a face and handed it over to the guide who accepted it gratefully. Once I ran out of filters, I bought the very prevalent and very cheap Marlboros.

At 2pm we reached Serenkot, 1592 metres high at the top of the mountain that overlooks Pokhara 700 metres below, and enjoyed a late lunch and a welcome rest in a restaurant. On one side the mountains filled the horizon; on the other the wide Pokhara valley stretched below, with Lake Phewa and the town in the distance.

We couldn't stay for long as the steep climb down to the valley had to be tackled before dark. This was even harder than the ascent the day before because every muscle hurt, every bone ached and I had developed a huge blister on one foot. Dumpling was in tears and weaving so much that she must have trebled the distance down. Another of the girls, who I called Sinead after the Irish singer, as she had a shaved head, twisted her knee and had to cling on to the guide. Even little Rajis had long stopped singing.

An exhausted, hobbling group, we finally reached the bottom, where I would gladly have swapped every possession for a ride back into town. But no taxi awaited on the second day of the strike and we trudged the last few miles into Pokhara, too tired to do more than nod goodbye when the Koreans took a different path.

On the way back, Rajis insisted we stop for chai in a café where he knew the people, wanting to show off that he'd led what was unquestionably his first trek. Whether a grubby, haggard, limping, middle-aged English woman was a good advert for his trekking prowess was questionable. The hot, sweet liquid was enough to get me to the hotel, where I just managed to hand over to Rajis what I hoped was a good tip before opening my room door and falling on the bed.

I wanted to remonstrate with the hotel manager that he hadn't had to pay for a proper guide or two taxis and had nearly killed me, but I didn't have the energy. After the best hot shower of my life, I sank into bed.

∞

What seemed like two minutes later, I was shaken awake by the alarm screaming in my ear. I turned blearily over. It was 6am. Having to get up for the early morning bus was bad enough, finding that my legs wouldn't work was worse but

Prize – India – Nepal – Singapore

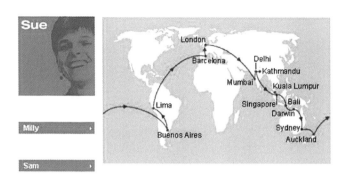

The Journey

Setting Off

Udaipur

Camel Safari

Jaisalnmer

Jaipur - Palace of the Winds

Taj Mahal

Varanasi

Kathmandu

Bruce taking a break from the valley (background) we walked

Nyatapola Temple, Bhaktapur

With Raji in the Annapurnas

Annapurnas

Singapore Quay

Bruce relaxing at Raffles

most disastrous was the state of my digestion. The chicken/baby poo had come home to roost and the thought of tackling the seven-hour bus journey back to Kathmandu whilst in the throes of my first serious case of diarrhoea wasn't an appealing one. I hastily swallowed an Imodium tablet and prayed it would stopper me up until Kathmandu – and would act quickly.

My taxi to the bus station didn't turn up and I had to hobble to the end of the road and beg to squeeze into one that was picking up a couple of Norwegian girls. I spent so long in the toilet at the station that someone started banging on the door. I just made it onto the bus on time, only to realise I'd left my sleeping bag in the wash room, and made the bus and its impatient passengers wait while I retrieved it.

The following seven hours have been blotted out of my memory. I only recall nearly being sick when a dish of dal bhat was placed in front of me for lunch. But without any mishaps – god bless Imodium – I was safely back in Kathmandu, The Star and bed.

∞

I was proud of my trek despite sore muscles that made me walk like John Wayne but with no one to listen to the tale, the loneliness of New Year's Eve returned. Was there any point in travelling to these exotic places when there was no one to share the experience with, no one to compare aches with or kiss on the stroke of midnight? Was I to spend the next four months conversing with a teddy bear, wasting away as I couldn't stand the local food? Would I ever laugh again now that Carol and Mike had gone, or was it to be all lonely and low? If so, I wasn't sure I could endure it.

Suddenly I remembered that tucked inside the case of my daughter Rachel's tape was a note with the strict instruction 'Only to be read when feeling sad or lonely.' That moment had arrived; I wrapped myself in a blanket ready to be comforted by her words.

I'd brought six tapes with me but the five I dug out of my

bag didn't include Rachel's with its precious note. I emptied the bag, throwing its carefully organised contents across the floor in an increasingly urgent frenzy, searching all its nooks and crannies – first aid pocket, spare battery supply, hidden flap with secret stash of dollars, map pocket. I'd rummaged through everything several times but all to no avail. At that moment what my daughter had written seemed the most important thing in the world and I had lost it. It was as if a thread that connected me with home was severed, leaving me adrift, alone and exiled. I wept.

Would I last six months? Normally I was happy with my own company, almost to the point of shutting out the rest of the world, but in six weeks I was already learning that being on your own and being lonely are very different things. That night, so far away from anything and anyone familiar, I wanted to beg or scream for someone to talk to me and, even better, hold me.

∞

That evening was a turning point. I knew now that to survive I had to learn how to 'backpack' – to shed my natural reserve and ignore the fact that I was thirty years older than everyone else. The following evening, after yet another solo meal in a café, I resolved to begin. Taking a deep breath, I attached myself to a group of young backpackers of assorted nationalities. I was made welcome and stayed chatting until late in the evening.

Buoyed up by this success, I struck up a conversation at breakfast the following morning with a French girl, Valerie, and we spent the next couple of days together. This was much more like I'd hoped travelling on my own would be.

I was just beginning to get the hang of this backpacking business when it was time to move on. Despite a few bad moments, I left Nepal feeling optimistic that it was going to be alright – I would make it.

∞

To rejoin my route, which would take me to Singapore, I had to fly back to Mumbai. Sitting next to me on the plane from Kathmandu was a tiny, ancient Nepalese woman with a face as wrinkled as a dried walnut. But her eyes, little black kernels, were full of excitement and curiosity as she craned to look past me out of the window. She tucked into the lunch of tasteless chicken, sticky rice, bright yellow blancmange and sweaty cheese with gusto. Not having a common language, we could only communicate by smiles and gestures and she tutted, shaking a skeletal finger at my discarded pudding. I wanted to warn her not to bite into the pat of margarine that she had carefully unwrapped but was too late and I tutted back, this time in sympathy, as she gulped down water. I felt an affinity with her – two women on an adventure late in our lives.

Mumbai had been an overwhelming place to start my journey but when I returned six weeks later, the dirt and smell seemed utterly normal and the beggars and touts were easily brushed aside with a mere wave of the arm. Had my demeanour and attitude changed that much? Certainly I didn't feel the same woman who'd quaked as she stepped out of the hotel on that first day. I'd learnt three key lessons about travelling: give off an air of confidence whatever is going on inside; say 'no' politely but firmly and, most important of all, keep smiling whatever incomprehensible mayhem is going on around you.

I had twenty-four hours to kill before my next flight and was meeting my first website contacts for dinner. Without a guidebook for India, I'd borrowed one from a backpacker and written down the address of a hotel near to our rendezvous point.

'Sorry, full up,' said the manager with an apologetic shrug. It had never occurred to me that hotels could be full and I was flummoxed.

'Please not to be worrying!' exclaimed the manager. 'My cousin good hotel having very close.' He summoned a porter, whose smile vanished when he felt the weight of my bag, unaware it had wheels.

Back on the street, we crossed a couple of roads and turned a corner into an alley ankle-deep in filth. The light was fading rapidly and the shady figures lurking in doorways assumed a menacing aspect in the gloom. My anxiety increased with every step, peaking as we waded through heaps of refuse towards a hole in the wall which was in fact a lift entrance.

Where in hell are we going, I wondered as the rickety, smelly lift began its juddering ascent. Just because he was skinny and not covered in scars and tattoos, it didn't mean the boy wasn't a kidnapper or pimp for the white slave trade. The lift stopped and we stepped out, not into a bandits' den but the foyer of a hotel. Any relief was short-lived, however, as after one sniff of the air and a glance at the seedy manager and his collection of grubby rooms I retreated, pulling boy and bag back into the lift. Safely back on street level, I tipped the exhausted boy and sent him on his way.

With darkness falling, I stood at a busy crossroads with no idea of where I was going to sleep in this scary city. Two hours back in Mumbai and my smug newfound confidence ebbed away, leaving the frightened novice. A recce down one road didn't reveal any welcoming hotel lights or signs, so I returned to my starting point. Tired, lost and ready to dissolve into an hysterical heap, I felt a tap on my shoulder and heard the wonderful words: 'Hello, Sue!'

My rescuers were my email dinner dates, Steve and Bobbie from Devon. Disorientated and thanks to no judgement on my part, I was standing close to our meeting point at the allotted time. They took charge immediately, called a taxi, secured the last free room in their respectable hotel, waited while I had a quick wash and brush-up and took me out to dinner.

We went to the Taj, Mumbai's top hotel, built by a wealthy Indian after he was refused entry into a whites-only colonial hotel. I'd been offered a room here through the website at the hugely discounted price of $299 a night, a nice gesture that I reluctantly turned down. The fact that I had nothing smart to wear was as big a consideration as the money. Now, in one of the many strange coincidences of this trip, here I was in the plush dining room where the glass chandelier tinkled, the starched tablecloth crackled, cutlery gleamed, and a besuited waiter hovered.

As there were only two tables in use in the dining room and I'd changed into the smarter of my trousers with a clean shirt, I didn't feel too underdressed, and tucked into a delicious masala dosa – curry inside a crisp pancake. Steve and Bobbie, a pair of wandering musicians well-travelled from cabaret gigs on cruise ships, were good company, and it was an enjoyable evening.

Back in the clean and safe hotel room, I settled down to sleep reflecting what a lucky person I was. Six weeks ago, without Steve and Bobbie, Carol, a taste of backpacking and coping with the odd riot or two, this evening's experience could have sent me home.

4

Sanitary Matters

I knew only three facts about my next stop, Singapore: it was very clean; my nephew lived there, and he had a spare room.

Stepping off the plane at Singapore was like walking into a sauna wearing a fur coat. The humidity, even at 7.30 in the morning, was overpowering and very different from the dry heat of India. By the time I reached the bottom of the aircraft steps, sweat was oozing from surfaces I hadn't been aware had pores. I hoped that my nephew, Dan, wouldn't mind his aunt being a little damp around the edges.

Despite the passing of twelve years, Dan was instantly recognisable. Besides looking similar to my son Ben, they also seem to share a penchant for the life and women of the East and an unwillingness to live in England. Maybe they also share a desire to escape the watchful eyes of their mothers.

The thirty-year-old man who met me was not the same boy my sister had worried about at eighteen. The good manners and cleanliness of Singapore had obviously been a good influence as Dan, now a respectable engineer, led me towards his Volvo. Inside the air-conditioned saloon, I thought I'd been transported to another world, with upmarket cars driving sedately along in clearly defined lanes, not a horn to be heard or rickshaw to be seen. Was this still Asia?

Later, I shyly asked if the paper could be flushed down the toilet. It could – and yes, you could also drink the water. We arranged to meet later and Dan went off to keep Singapore supplied with all the forklift trucks it needed to keep the shelves of its well-oiled economy stocked.

Only those who have spent a month squatting over Asian toilets can imagine the pleasure of sitting on a proper toilet with a plentiful supply of soft paper to hand. Gone was the struggle to find the least-flooded spot before balancing bag and body in the unaccustomed squatting position, trying to keep trousers and shoes out of harm's way. There was no need for contortions to extricate paper from pocket or bag without falling over, not to mention the problem of disposal, as to put it down the hole would guarantee further flooding. I knew the hose or bucket of water was there to avoid this problem and the left hand was involved, but this was one local custom I was not going to try, especially as I was left- or cack-handed, a term that had taken on a whole new meaning. Dan's loo, together with a shower, followed by a bed with crisp clean sheets and a quietly efficient air-con system, made me feel like I'd died in Bombay and been reincarnated in one of those pink Hindu heavens painted on the sides of Indian buses.

Early evening, I met Dan at the riverside, a cosmopolitan area of bars and restaurants full of Singapore's willowy young trendsetters, whose gym-toned bodies had been expensively wrapped in the latest designer creations. The skyscrapers of the financial district loomed around us, the smattering of lights still burning, pinpricks of conscience to those Singaporeans who dared to leave the office before midnight. 'Work hard' seemed to be the philosophy of the Singaporeans, 70% of whom were of Chinese origin, 'drink hard' that of the expats. Entering Dan's local, an Irish bar, was like being beamed back to a London pub on a Friday night, with inebriated Brits – interspersed with a few Aussies – shouting, sweating, staggering, singing and gulping down vast quantities of chilled beer. Walking back later with Dan, we passed a florist's.

'Look at that,' said Dan proudly. 'Where else would you see pots of plants and flowers outside a closed shop? They won't be stolen or vandalised either.'

'Yeah, great,' I said. This adult, law-abiding Dan, who was moved by pots of flowers, was strangely unnerving.

∞

For the next few days I wandered round this hot, humid peninsula where cramming 4.5 million people onto 700 square kilometres means building vertically. The skyscrapers looked like a dense three-dimensional bar chart patterned with pixilated windows and capped with cranes pushing the bars ever higher. To keep the city clean, urinating in public, spitting and chewing gum have all been declared heinous crimes by the powers that be, while smoking in public places was also forbidden – and heaven preserve you if you dropped a gum wrapper or cigarette butt on the street.

The wide roads, flanked on all sides by tall, gleaming shopping malls and offices, led me to the famous shopping paradise of Orchard Street. On either side of the tree-lined boulevard, a solid phalanx of malls within malls within yet more malls awaited the crowds of dedicated shoppers laden down with designer bags from designer shops.

Rare among women, I hate shopping and had no intention of spending time in Marks & Spencer's, Robinsons or even Takashimayas. My daughter, Rachel, when forced through poverty to take me with her to the shops, knows she must seize maximum advantage in the first hour before the bored glaze and the pull of coffee shops ends all hope of the purse strings opening. Even Singapore's Chinatown was neat and tidy – still colourful, but without the steam and mayhem. I walked on to Raffles, the legendary colonial hotel famed for its gin slings but, as it was early afternoon, the bar was deserted.

An exhibition of Chinese art and crafts in the Raffles Shopping Centre across the road tempted me. It was Rachel's birthday the next day and I still hadn't sent off her birthday parcel. I looked up our Chinese birth years at a stall selling pendants: mine was the year of the ox, which might explain my lack of dancing ability, and Rachel's was the year of the cock. Without dwelling on what that might signify, I bought her a pendant, which was quite enough shopping for me.

More interesting than the Singapore shops were the taxi

drivers who, without exception, were eager to talk and seemed to be obsessed with the UK news, or at least a Chinese-whispers' version.

'How is the Queen, is she well?' asked one elderly driver.

'Fine, the last time I saw her,' I replied.

'What do you think about Scotland now that it is independent?' said a glamorous lady taxi driver with shades and black leather driving gloves.

Baffled by where this one had come from, I ignored it as it was too hot to go into the intricacies of Scottish governance. Once the news was dealt with, there came the inevitable question: 'Where is your husband?' At first I had answered honestly, saying that I was divorced, but when met with incomprehension, embarrassment or deepest sympathy, it was simpler to just lie and say he was at home.

Another thing I learnt to my cost about Singapore taxi drivers is that at 9pm they all go home for dinner, and will only take you if your destination is on their route home. After a hard day wandering in the energy-sapping humidity, I ate at the riverside but gave up on the long taxi queue and set off on foot, trying to hail a taxi as I walked. A couple of cars stopped but shook their heads at Dan's address that he'd written on a piece of paper.

Trying to read the guidebook map's tiny print under the dim streetlights was impossible and I soon became hopelessly lost. I found myself wandering beside a dual carriageway, then behind a row of offices and finally through an estate of flats. No taxis here. I wasn't afraid in safe Singapore, just exhausted and cross with myself for not having the patience to queue.

Eventually I stumbled back onto Orchard Road, found a driver who'd finished his dinner, and arrived back at 11.30pm to find Dan anxiously pacing up and down, wondering how he would explain that he'd lost his newly found aunt.

∞

The following day I sent my first parcel home, which included Rachel's present. My last child was now twenty and all those turbulent teenage years were finally over. The inevitable tantrums and moody sulks with accusations of, 'Everyone else's mother is letting them go,' 'No one else has to be in that early,' etc, etc, had been replaced by actual conversations. Rachel was tearful when I rang to wish her happy birthday and I felt another pang of mother-guilt at abandoning my children for six months. Rachel had been born with overactive tear ducts and, cowed by two older brothers, had spent most of her childhood clinging to my legs. Only three months ago I'd left her weeping at a college in Devon and now I was swanning round the world, even renting out her bedroom to a lodger. She was supposed to stay with her father but I heard from my email spies that, when home, she spent more time dossing on the couch in what had become Ely's top party venue. At least this time the line was good and I could tell her how much I loved and missed her.

Shopping and post done, it was time for Singapore's tourist attractions. First was a river trip in a 'bumboat', a flat-bottomed barge now used to ferry tourists rather than goods. It was pleasant floating past the riverside areas of restaurants and clubs, including the Quay where Raffles landed, as far as the Merlion statue – a bizarre nine-metre-high effigy of a lion's head on a fish's bottom that guards the entrance to the river. But throughout the journey a perfectly synchronised pre-recorded commentary emanated from speakers on the boat, which I found intensely irritating.

Next was Sentosa, 'Island of Many Pleasures'. It is Singapore's top holiday spot, a cross between Disneyland and Centre Parcs, containing themed attractions such as Fort Siloso and VolcanoLand, sport at Sijori WonderGolf and a replica Merlion with a lift inside. The cable car to the island from Mount Faber gave views of the docks, oil silos and rows of tankers on the horizon but, as it was quite early the island was deserted, all bars and cafés shut. After walking through the very tidy jungle nature trail, I ambled along the beach made of imported sand. Everything, including the rocks, was labelled. The monorail featured the inevitable commentary, so I decided I'd had enough of Sentosa Island and caught a taxi back to Dan's. The sanitised cleanliness of Singapore was oddly disturbing and I was ready to move on from tidiness, skyscrapers and monorails back to 'normal' bustling, chaotic Asia.

On my last night, Dan and I went out for a meal to a Mexican restaurant where he persuaded me to try margaritas, which arrived by the jug-full and were drunk from jam jars. Dan, well into his jam jar, became nostalgic about home and his mother, my sister Jen, long divorced from his father, Dave.

'I mish my mum most,' he rambled tipsily. 'I want her to come here on a holiday but she's gone and married a second Dave.'

'Djer know,' I said, 'your mum's called Jennifer but second Dave has "Linda" tattooed on one set of knuckles.'

'Course I know she called Jennifer,' answered Dan.

Deciding that margaritas dulled the mind, and aware that I'd not packed yet, I opted to go back rather than party on with Dan. He hadn't returned when it was time for me to leave in the morning, giving me hope that the old Dan-fire survives under the surface.

Singapore was a pleasant place for a few days' rest but I was ready to move on into Malaysia, keen to try some jungle in its provinces on Borneo.

5

Rainforest Romance

This diversion to Borneo, famous for orang-utans and wild head-hunters, felt like a real adventure. I was alone without a tour leader or relative to help – but actually, this wasn't quite true as I did have Uncle Steven. After Amanda, my son Ben's girlfriend, said she had Chinese-Malay relations in Kuching, Sarawak, on the north of the Indonesian island of Borneo, I'd emailed Uncle Steven with the message: 'Hello, I'm Sue, your niece's boyfriend's mother,' and had been invited to stay.

As I stood in the arrivals area of the airport, the only foreigner and the only person who hadn't been met by relative or taxi driver, my heart sank. Where was Uncle Steven? Suddenly, a waving figure burst into the airport, hastily introduced himself as Steven, shook my hand and, although slight of build and a head shorter than me, effortlessly picked up my bag and swept me off into his car that contained two shy children.

Steven did everything, including talking and driving, at high speed, impatient with any delay. He gallantly brushed aside my cultural faux pas when I forgot to take off my shoes before entering his house. Oh, to live in a climate where all that covered the window spaces was ornate wrought iron, with no need for glass!

That first evening we broke the ice with a stroll along the riverside in Kuching, a walkway adorned with coloured fountains, little gardens and kiosks. Kuching was a quiet, relaxed city, without the skyscrapers of Singapore or the frenzy and pollution of the Indian conurbations. We stopped to watch a concert of Chinese music played on an assortment of strange instruments that appeared to be constructed out of orange boxes and bits of driftwood. The musicians, with bony bodies and thin, straggly beards, were all octogenarians at the very least.

'Unfortunately, the young aren't interested in hearing or playing traditional music,' Steven said. 'Eventually, it will die.' Sooner rather than later, I thought sadly, as time for these musicians looked to be running out fast.

Children are the same all over the world, and I won instant favour by buying Steven's four – Cesar, Cheryl, Ben and Daryl – an ice-cream each. They could speak a little English, much of it learnt from the endless American cartoons on the television. Steven spoke excellent English as he'd been a student in London and enjoyed relating how he survived.

'I would go to the butcher's and they would give me the organs and entrails of chickens. Here we consider those parts to be delicacies and I couldn't understand why you Westerners threw them out.'

I was tucking into a delicious curry that his wife, Jennifer, had made until Steven asked, 'Are you enjoying the chicken feet?'

∞

I was treated to another slice of Chinese food and culture the next morning when Steven took me for breakfast in a typical Chinese eating-house. To me it felt more like a Turkish bath full of hyperactive brokers than a café. Chopsticks and conversation moved at an amazing speed, creating waves of noise, steam and bustle. Steven had free rein to order my food and I was presented with a bowl of a soupy mixture full of strange blobs. Two lumps identified themselves as chicken and liver but the rest will forever remain a mystery, which is probably just as well. My drink was a bowl of crushed ice sprinkled with unfamiliar bits of grain and seeds that looked like the scrapings from the bottom of a freezer.

Later, with a sadistic glint in his eye, Steven insisted that I try Malaysia's favourite fruit, durian. The night market was crowded with Malay families picking at piles of what looked like prickly medicine balls, earnestly sniffing, caressing and testing the weight of individual fruit, as if they were choosing a child to adopt. After much careful consideration, our lucky durian was paid for and taken back to the house, where the children danced with excitement as Steven broke it open. As a foul smell filled the kitchen, I was reminded of Cambridge sewage works on a hot day. But the children dived into the white sticky pulp inside, scooping out the gooey substance by the handful and shovelling it into their mouths. Out of politeness I tried some on the end of a finger, only to find that it tasted as bad as it smelt.

'Don't worry,' laughed Steven. 'Very few Westerners like it. In fact, Amanda's father is the only Englishman I have ever met who does.'

'Well, he is a psychiatrist,' I said, wondering how anyone could like cat-poo-scented marshmallow.

Once the children had gorged themselves, we settled down to a game of Monopoly on a board featuring the streets of Kuala Lumpur. Steven, a Chinese businessman dealing in timber, played Monopoly with the same competitiveness and risk-taking as in life. After he forced his ten-year-old daughter into bankruptcy and mortgaged everything to put hotels on streets I was approaching, I believed his boast that he'd never lost a game of Monopoly. He won, of course.

∞

I spent the next day wandering around shops full of wooden artefacts and carved animals, and visited the cultural museum, which housed replicas of various styles of longhouses – communal wooden barn-like buildings raised on stilts above boggy ground. Young men and women dressed in traditional costumes met me at each house and presented displays of weaving, cooking and dancing. My attempt at using a blowpipe was woeful, my dart missing the board by a metre. The authenticity of the experience was tarnished when a man carving a round-backed, guitar-like instrument offered to play one he had made earlier and plugged it into an amplifier.

Steven was even more like a coiled spring at dinner. Once the little ones had been taken off to bed he announced, 'I have a big surprise. I am taking you and Cesar to a Chinese trance session.'

As we set off in the car, I whispered to Cesar, Steven's eldest son, 'Have you been to one of these before? Do you know what happens?'

'No, first time,' Cesar whispered back.

We drove to a temple – the converted house of one who has been chosen by the gods – slipped off our shoes and joined the crowd lighting handfuls of incense at the various shrines. Steven showed me the ranks of statues of gods around the walls, which seemed a confusing mixture of Chinese images and Hindu deities.

'Look! Touch!' he ordered, showing me the large nails protruding upwards through the seat and arms of a chair. I gingerly brushed the top of the sharp points.

'The holy man will sit there. Look underneath!' Steven pointed at the razor-sharp blade where the feet rested. I asked Steven the purpose of this ceremony but he wasn't interested in the finer detail.

'I just cover all the odds: I pray to Islam in mosques and to Hindu and Chinese gods in whichever temple I find myself.'

Expecting an ancient, hairy holy man, I was surprised when a small, muscular young man, wearing only a pair of yellow nylon shorts, arrived to begin his preparations. I was sitting on a bench opposite the shrine to the elephant god Ganash, the sole Hindu god that was represented, when I was politely asked to move, as this was tonight's chosen god and apparently women shouldn't sit in front of such a deity. Feeling like a conspicuous elephant myself among these small people, I quickly changed places with Cesar.

The ceremony started with men smashing coconuts as

they asked for their luck to change, covering the floor with sticky milk that mingled with the water and mud from the tropical rain lashing down outside that sloshed around my bare feet. The young man entered his trance, shaking ever more violently while emitting elephant noises and strange cries that his band of followers tried to interpret.

As the trumpeting got louder, I had a terrible urge to giggle but this disappeared when the holy man started working a large steel hook through his cheek. Transfixed along with the rest of the audience, I watched the hook being inched slowly through his cheek; sweat – but no blood – trickled down his face, which was blank with no sign of pain. Gradually, as the other end appeared in his open mouth, the strangled noises and mumbled cries became louder until he pulled out the hook and fainted.

Caught by his attentive followers, he was guided to sit upon the chair of nails. After much mumbling of their own, it became clear to them which god had entered the young man, whereupon they dressed him in the appropriate robes. He slowly came round, assisted by a mug of beer and a cigar. Puffing and sipping, he blessed amulets to give to the people queuing for favours. Abruptly, it was over and we left, with shoes now on sticky feet.

'Why didn't you take any photographs?' asked Steven, slightly put out.

'It didn't feel appropriate.'

Never having felt more of a foreigner in an alien world, I hadn't wanted to click away with the camera.

'Well, what did you think of the trance?' Steven quizzed.

'I don't know,' I answered lamely.

Although I'd touched the nails, seen the hook go through the cheek and shared the absorption of the audience, I didn't understand any of it. Despite being put off religion for life by my Catholic upbringing, I'd occasionally dabbled in the mystic or mysterious, participating in a bit of levitation while a student, and having my past lives examined by a friend who was heavily into angels. But the Chinese trance session baffled me and I wasn't surprised to learn that Cesar was up all night with nightmares.

∞

Having sampled the delights of Chinese food and religion, Steven helped me organise a trip to Bako National Park to lose my rainforest virginity. I caught a little motorised boat from the village of Kampung Bako to the park further up the coast. After an exhilarating and bumpy twenty-minute ride across a choppy sea, the park came into view – rich green jungle as far as the eye could see, gnarled mangrove trees growing out of the water, rocky cliffs with bays of golden sand, turquoise sea and not a human in sight.

After landing at the tiny jetty and checking in at the park office, a ranger took me to the hostel – 'basic but clean' in guidebook jargon – and I was given a four-bed dorm to myself. The windows were covered with mesh and the ranger warned me that anything lying around would be purloined by the impudent macaque monkeys who preyed on the camp.

At the information centre I studied the maps of the walking trails, choosing the Lintang Loop, which was supposed to take three to four hours. So, armed only with a bottle of water, a bag of buns and a sun hat, this fifty-one-year-old truant-catcher from the flat Fens strode off into the jungle, scrambling up a narrow trail strewn with rocks, roots and creepers. I was deep in the jungle within minutes, climbing cliffs giving views over forested hills, peering into the dense alien vegetation, listening to the loud, high-pitched whine of cicadas, wading through abundant little streams trickling over rocks and pushing my way through tangles of dangling vines.

I didn't meet another soul and didn't want to. I was absorbed in discovering a new world, imagining I was Margaret Mead, Livingstone and Indiana Jones rolled into one. With sweat trickling down my face, back and everywhere else, mud covering my trusty walking boots and much of my legs, I strode on with a beatific smile. It didn't matter that I didn't know the names of the tall, majestic trees, the ferns, creepers and plants – it was enough to enjoy the green lushness of the whole package.

After an hour, the thick forest opened up into a sandstone plateau with large red rocks divided by gullies full of the red water that was a feature of Borneo. I sat on a large boulder to rest, take deep draughts of water, munch on a bun and soak in the experience. This was all I'd hoped for in travelling: to be somewhere so different from my normal life. Feeling like a child allowed out on its own for the first time, I was glad to be alone, the experience untainted by anyone else's perceptions, and felt ridiculously happy. The only worry was that I had less than half my water left and serious rationing had to begin.

The trail led deeper and deeper into the jungle, where huge buttress roots stretched out to balance the long trunks that grew upward in the search for light. These roots grew out of the trunk above ground, arching themselves before diving under the forest floor, leaving hollow caves underneath the trunk. Some were smooth and flat like rudders or whales' tails, others resembled giant spiders' legs.

I was so absorbed in these strangely shaped tangles that I only gradually became aware that the continuous hum and chirrup of the insects had stopped and the light was dimming. In the depths of the forest, the earth, rocks and plants became mossy, dark, dense and dripping, and the air heavy and damp. I stopped walking, awed by this silent, ageless jungle, so primitive, so fertile, so untamed. As this primeval world took me in, an entirely new peace overcame me as if I was the only person in the world and nothing outside here and now existed. I held my breath, afraid to disturb this moment. I could have stayed there all day but, as tiredness and dehydration forced themselves into my consciousness, I moved on.

With all the rests and digressions, the three hours the trail was meant to take had stretched into six and reluctantly I began to hurry. The guidebook warned that the visitor isn't likely to see the rare proboscis monkeys that live on Bako in the daytime, but when I heard crashing in the trees above, I knew something was heading my way. Standing absolutely still, I watched a troop pass through the canopy above, grey shapes swinging from branch to branch in a smooth rhythm. They were so high up in the tall trees that I could only just make out the strange pendulous noses but that was enough – my cup ran over (although my water bottle remained empty).

Tired but elated, I reached the camp and bought a large bottle of water, downing half of it in huge gulps. Evening was approaching and amidst deafening thunder and impressive lightning, the heaviest tropical storm I'd yet witnessed exploded around me. After sprinting to the café for a plate of chicken rice, I returned to my room to find that all that was left of the two buns I'd saved for breakfast was the bag, untied, not ripped, and a few crumbs on the floor. Who or what had feasted on my buns, and how had they got in? Above the meshed window I noticed some extremely narrow slats that only a snake, lizard, spider or very small and supple monkey could squeeze through. Snakes and spiders don't have fingers to untie the bag, lizards' arms are too short, so it had to be the monkey. A last sweep of the room confirmed that it was now free of all wildlife and I sank into bed, tired from one of the best days of my life.

∞

My week in Sarawak was over but, craving more rainforest, I delayed my flight to Kuala Lumpur and left Kuching to head north to more national parks. I wanted to go by river but Steven insisted it was too dangerous at this time of year and bundled me onto the bus for the much longer seven-hour journey to the halfway point at Sibu.

Although the bus was reasonably comfortable, my problem was with the stops. I was the only foreigner and nobody spoke English, so when we stopped at a café I followed the driver like a lost puppy, pointing anxiously at my watch and raising my hands questioningly. He merely shrugged his shoulders and sat down for his meal, dismissing me as if swatting away an irritating fly.

After two stops I began to understand the pattern: a meal

of some sort would be waiting for the two drivers and we would stay as long as it took them to eat it, then it was a loud blast of the horn and off we went without a head count. Terrified of the bus driving off without me, I established my own pattern: leaping off at the stop, rushing to the front of the loo queue and buying a bag of crisps or biscuits rather than risk ordering anything to eat. That was my food for the day.

At Sibu, I checked into a hotel above a row of shops. I'd chosen it from the 'budget' list in the guidebook, choosing words like 'friendly' and 'clean' alongside the inevitable 'basic'. The descriptions were usually pretty accurate and this room justified all three adjectives but with the addition of 'wet', as not only did the shower empty onto the floor, which was usual, but the wash basin did too. Luckily I'd taken the advice of a well-travelled Australian emailer who wrote, 'You don't know who or what has been there before you' and had bought a pair of flip-flops.

By now it was getting dark and I was ravenous but the cafés appeared to lack menus and people just shouted something as they sat down and a dish was brought to them. Afraid that if I tried to imitate them I would be presented with a bowl full of fish or chicken entrails, I played safe and bought some noodles and satay from a street stall, which I ate with a beer in a little bar.

∞

It's said that there are two groups of people in the world: night people and morning people. I am firmly in the former camp and slept so late that I missed the boat trip Steven had suggested for my day in Sibu. I ambled around the narrow streets instead, with two rows of stalls in front of the shops. I didn't see another Westerner all day and my face ached with smiling in response to the many curious stares of the locals.

Down to my last loo roll, the main task was to buy another. That proved so difficult that I was convinced that Malays must disguise them to avoid embarrassment. At last I spotted one free with a large pack of disposable nappies, and so began the tortuous process of trying to explain to the assistant that I didn't have a six-month-old baby hidden away in my rucksack, neither was I yet incontinent, but I did want the toilet roll – by now quite desperately. She finally seemed to grasp what one finger pointing to the loo roll and one finger raised seemed to mean and scuttled off, returning with a triumphant smile and one pack of ten rolls. I didn't have the heart to disappoint her and bought the lot.

That took care of my evening, which was spent removing the cardboard tubes and squashing as many rolls as possible into the crevices of my bag – one in my wash bag (not a good idea as it swiftly became papier-mâché), two with the medicines, another two with the dirty washing bag (hmm – would I fancy using them later?) and the last few mangled up in the various pockets. When not another square inch could be found, I tried, unsuccessfully, to put the middles back in the remaining three to donate them to the hotel.

∞

The six-hour bus ride from Sibu to Miri, an oil town on the edge of the South China Sea and the Sungai Miri River, was very similar to the Kuching-to-Sibu trip the day before, with anxious stops and broken biscuits. When a young Malay girl got on halfway and sat next to me, I offered her one of my battered biscuits but she politely shook her head.

When we got back on the bus after a short stop, she presented me with several bags of chopped fruit, a little packet of hot chick peas and a bunch of spiky red balls that looked like conkers. The biscuits were consigned to the bin and my companion obviously enjoyed watching me as I tucked into this feast of new tastes and textures. Though we had no common language, she seemed to understand when I thanked her – as well as laughing when I couldn't find a way into the conker.

'Rambutan,' she said, demonstrating how to open one with a sharp twist, exposing the lychee-like fruit inside. If this was what I got every time I offered someone a biscuit, I resolved to do it more often.

What never ceased to surprise and delight me on this trip was the kindness of ordinary people. Another such act came from Jeremy and Gay, an expat, semi-retired couple resident in Miri, who had contacted me by email and arrived at my hotel to take me out to dinner.

'I have a surprise,' said Jeremy when we were in the car. 'Listen to this!' he said, turning on the radio.

'Traffic news – we have an accident in on the Hammersmith Flyover, expect delays. After Robbie Williams, it's Capital Radio's weekly roundup of gigs in London this weekend...' A disembodied DJ had joined us from London.

'One of the sons of the Sultan of Brunei, just north of here, had Capitol Radio beamed out to Brunei when he returned from university in England,' Jeremy explained. 'We often listen – it's a little piece of home.'

The image of this couple jigging away to the charts in the middle of Borneo was bizarre.

The tour of Miri didn't take long. It was formerly little more than a rest place for oil workers and a jumping-off point for Sarawak's other national parks but had expanded rapidly to accommodate glitzy malls and (plans for) a riverside recreation area. In fact, not much was open as the ten-day Chinese New Year was just starting and everyone was heading home. We watched a Chinese dragon dance at a hotel – I still don't understand why the orange peel is spat out – and after a curry we stopped off at their bungalow. Relaxing in an armchair reading the paper, it was so normal and so like home that for an evening I forgot I was in a faraway land.

∞

Mulu National Park can only be reached by air. At the tiny wooden airport I wandered out to the landing strip to take a picture of my transport, a twin-engine Otter. The plane flew so low over the land that I could see clearly the swathes of dense jungle, broken only by a red river snaking through it, and the occasional ugly bare scar where the loggers had been.

Apart from one English family, the plane was full of Malays returning home for the Chinese New Year.

A large taxi was waiting for the English family, obviously booked into the big, plush Royal Mulu Hotel across the river. My transport to the much humbler park accommodation was a battered jeep driven by a young man with one arm. Not needing a second arm nor wanting any conversation, he managed the rough, winding track with consummate ease and dropped me at the park.

This was my first experience of a hostel dormitory and it was a shock to find that the one large room was inhabited by both sexes. Affecting a nonchalant and experienced air, I slung my bag on a bed and introduced myself to the two young lads lounging on their beds in their underpants. A group of English girls on voluntary gap-year projects arrived shortly afterwards and we all went out to eat. It felt good to return to those last days in Nepal, spending my time with groups of youngsters of assorted nationalities, accepted as just another backpacker, my age of no consequence. Luckily I love chicken rice, as that seemed to be the standard fare in the parks.

At bedtime, I was overcome by an adolescent shyness. How does one change? Does everyone just strip off? Though desperate for sleep, I pretended to read and peeked out from behind the book to see what the others were doing, hoping not to be caught out and thought of as a pervert. The youngsters chatted on, oblivious to my need for guidance until, at last, they also tired and settled down to sleep in their daytime T-shirts and pants. My clothes were just too grubby to sleep in and I felt a middle-aged need to change out of them. Sod it, I thought, and went into the shower to don my cotton nightie, ignoring a stifled giggle from one of the girls.

∞

After breakfast the boys went out and the English girls were leaving, so I set off to explore Mulu on my own. This park was much wetter than Bako; the only paths were boardwalks, although the boggy ground didn't bother the Borneo bearded pigs. Large boars with browny-grey, bristly skin, their elongated faces were adorned with Groucho-like moustaches and long, fleshy pink snouts permanently muddy from snuffling in the swampy water. They were the ugliest animals I'd ever seen; I felt sure they'd never been used as models for cuddly toys.

Both Mulu and the nearby park, Niah, are renowned for their large limestone caves, but a generator failure marred my day at the Mulu caves. With only a faint natural light from the hole at the top, and an inadequate Maglite torch, I scurried through Deer Cave, a cavern full of tortuous rock formations, bats and an overpowering smell of ammonia, unable to take in much of its majesty.

At the Lang Cave the pitch-black entrance was too much for my nerve and my baby torch, so I sat on a rock in the sun and waited for someone to come along. Prior to the trip I found it impossible to just sit still and do nothing. The simple act of waiting was a new experience for me, another step in learning not only to be a backpacker but in being prepared to ask for help. Normally I'd be off buying a new torch or organising the generator repair instead of just sitting quietly. My time wasn't wasted as I watched rainbow-coloured butterflies and tiny iridescent hummingbirds hovering over tropical flowers, and photographed a large snake that was sunning itself on the path.

Within an hour, a gang of eight young Malaysians armed with big torches and flashlights arrived. When I showed them my little light they laughed and invited me to accompany them. Visitors to the caves are asked to be quiet so as not to disturb the bats and birds, but my band giggled and shouted their way round as they admired the white stalactites and stalagmites that twisted and curved themselves into MC Escher-like shapes round the sides of the vast cavern.

I thanked my companions for allowing me to share their light, and settled with a book and a packet of monkey nuts at the bat observatory to await the famed nightly exodus of a reputed two million bats from the caves. It was getting dark, the usual time for the emergence of the bats passed and all but four of the waiting crowd were led away by their guides. Eventually a paltry few hundred bats drifted out of the caves in strings and doughnut-shaped groups, a token reward for our patience.

Back at the hostel, there had been an influx of visitors including an irascible older German lady with cropped grey hair and a weather-beaten face.

'My aunt likes to travel with Adventure Tours,' said a young English girl in conversation with a Belgian.

'Bah!' interjected the German. 'Tours are an expensive waste. Better to travel on your own.'

'My sister is in Bali now,' the Belgian replied, ignoring the comment.

'Bali is very over-rated.'

At that, the other residents left, inviting me to accompany them. On our way back from dinner, we passed the fraulein sitting alone in the park café and I persuaded the others to stop for a drink.

'I hear that you won a trip around a world with the Guardian. What did you have to do to win?' she asked.

'Write 500 words on why they should pick me,' I answered proudly.

'Hmph, is that all?' she snorted. 'The Guardian's standards must be slipping.'

'I'm tired,' I announced, getting up. 'I think I'll head for bed.'

∞

Most hostellers were off the next day to do the Pinnacle walk but Peter the Slovak, a super-fit experienced trekker, said that he'd found it difficult. That was enough for me and I walked to Clearwater Cave with Dave, a Canadian postman who kept fit by sprinting his round. When we had walked to the end of the path inside the huge cavern with a crystal-clear river running through it, Dave announced he was going to follow it, and I nervously watched him wade off until his torch was a mere dot. The wave of a ten-ringgit note was enough to coax one of the Royal Mulu boatmen into gesturing me into his long canoe – much to the surprise of the Japanese family already in it – and we went back up-river.

Back at the hostel, Peter asked who wanted to join him for coffee at the home of Willie, a leader of the local Berawan tribe. As we sat on his veranda, Willie explained that his mission in life was to spread the word about how his tribe had been tricked out of land so that developers could build the Royal Mulu Resort down the road.

'We agreed that some of our land can be national park but our chiefs were tricked out of twenty acres more for the hotel. Developers now want more land to build a golf course so that rich Japanese and Americans will come. Now they knock away big hills to make big airport.'

'What can you do to stop them?' asked Peter.

'Few years back, some men set fire to the park generators. I no do it, but I was arrested and beaten up,' Willie told us angrily. 'Then we go to the courts to say it's our land, we should be the ones to develop it, but nothing happens and now the machines knock down hills.'

'Sue's a journalist,' Peter proclaimed excitedly.

'You will tell the people in England?' said Willie, even more excited.

'I'll do my best,' I replied, not wanting to tell him that a mention in the travel section of the online Guardian was unlikely to spark widespread protest. The backpackers that he lobbied were, by their very nature, going to be sympathetic, but anyone influential would be staying at the Royal Mulu, so I guess he was onto a loser. He did get his mention in my report as promised and I was grateful to travel in this beautiful area before any further development had taken place.

My last evening at Mulu reminded me of my days as an anxious parent, not able to settle until the children were safely home. Dave finally reappeared at about ten o'clock saying he had had a great time.

∞

The biggest of the limestone caves was at Niah, a two-hour journey from Miri on a very rickety bus followed by a riverboat journey to the park HQ. The hostel here was luxurious – newly refurbished with polished wood and shiny tiles. The only other occupants were an English couple from Bolton and Klaus, an elderly German, so once again I had a four-bed dorm to myself.

Klaus had been there a couple of weeks, during which he'd gone native, going out every morning to harvest food. He was quite well-preserved for his age and had a little white beard that set off his deep tan.

If you rounded up all the men in my life the line may not be long – but it would be quite hairy, with an abundance of short beards. It would also include one large walrus moustache which, blinded by lust, I found attractive at the time.

I was happy to accept Klaus's gifts of fruits of the forest but declined that of his loins, implied in a request that I stay on here and keep him company. The fact that he mentioned he had both a wife and a girlfriend more than cancelled out the beard.

On the way to the main cave was a steep slope up to a view over the forest. After clambering three-quarters of the way up, I found myself slithering backwards down the slope. In an instinctive reaction, I locked my legs straight and leant forward, but was unable to halt the downward slide. The picture of this middle-aged woman travelling backwards as if going the wrong way on a ski slope would have been a sure winner in any home-movie programme. Arriving back on level ground, shaken but unharmed, I walked on to the Great Cave rather more carefully.

The entrance, a huge gaping mouth dribbling creepers and with teeth of jagged stalactites, led into an enormous cavern, where a squeaky cacophony of millions of bats and swifts filled the air. There were boardwalks, slippery with bat droppings, for visitors but the guano collectors, shy people who avoided the tourists, skipped about the rocks like mountain goats, their twinkling lamps dotting the cave.

My trusty boots weren't designed for this surface and, as my feet slid from under me, I found myself landing heavily on my backside. Two local children crystallised out of the darkness and shouted, but when I gestured I was OK they melted away once more. Having lost confidence on the treacherous surface, I shuffled along slowly clinging onto the guide ropes, which meant that both my hands and the seat of my shorts were now covered in acrid bat shit.

Occasionally I dared raise the torch to see the walls which, stained by minerals and guano and eroded by water, were like a fantasy world. Dotted about the cave were precarious-looking bamboo poles that disappeared towards the roof. They were used to collect the swifts' nests for the famous bird's nest soup, a lucrative but dangerous occupation. I've always wondered who would want to eat soup made of swift spit.

Emerging from the cave, I took the path that I thought headed back but it merely petered out. When a fierce tropical storm broke – hungry and thirsty, having used most of my water to wash my hands – I went back into the cave to retrace my steps. This meant renegotiating the boardwalk, made more slippery by the rainwater dripping off me.

Everyone else seemed to have disappeared and, for the first time on the trip, I was frightened of being alone. What if I slipped again and broke my leg, or lost my way, to be trapped in this cave forever? I inched my way back along what now seemed spooky paths; by the time I reached the entrance and daylight I was shaking.

Back in the forest the tropical storm was at its height. After buying a bunch of rambutan from a vendor anxious to clear her stock and go home, I sheltered under an overhanging rock that formed a cave and which had a small stream at the bottom. This was the first time I'd been aware of the potential danger and vulnerability of being on my own; until now, it hadn't crossed my mind that it might not be wise to tramp through jungle and caves alone.

Until I checked into an internet café to send in my weekly report or send emails, no one in the world knew where I was.

However, sitting in my little cave, twisting open the rambutan, watching the fat raindrops bounce off the dark foliage, turning to mist as they hit the hot earth, the fear melted away as once again I felt the rainforest wrap itself protectively around me. I had never felt any void since discarding religion, but twice now in the rainforest I'd experienced a powerful sense of being part of something inclusive, making me feel peaceful and content. I would have to be careful or I might start hugging trees.

As the storm showed no sign of passing, I reluctantly left the spot and carried on. Needing another rest, I stopped at a wooden shelter at the side of the path and was joined by a middle-aged Malay dressed only in shorts.

'I live in longhouse,' he announced, waving vaguely in a direction away from the path. 'You want to stay there, only fifty ringgits?'

'No thank you, I'm staying at the park.'

He looked at his wet feet and then lifted his head to stare me straight in the eye. 'You married?' he asked. 'I look for wife.'

'Husband at home,' I lied, laughing and he grinned too, shrugged and moved on. I would have loved to stay in a longhouse but wasn't prepared to pay fifty ringgits or get married for the privilege.

It was time for me to move on to mainland Malaysia – a pity, as Niah was obviously the place to go if you were looking for a man.

6

Festivals, Fortunes And Family

I sang to myself for comfort as I walked down a dark driveway that led to a gloomy, barrack-like building. Arriving in Kuala Lumpur at midnight, mindful of the experience of Mumbai, I'd taken the precaution of pre-booking a bed at the YWCA, surely a safe option in a strange city.

Before leaving home, one of my recurring nightmares had been a vision of a forlorn woman with a gigantic bag standing alone in a strange airport, weeping pitifully, with no idea how to find accommodation or transport. My fears had been unfounded as two generations of student travel had led to the 'backpacker bus', a wonderful service that dropped you off at your chosen accommodation. I wonder if Heathrow has one. The only other passenger on the bus from Kuala Lumpur airport was a young girl who, despite the obligatory torn jeans and big rucksack, was dropped off at a glitzy hotel complete with uniformed bellboy and line of classy motors. No roughing it here.

There was no smart bellboy to greet me; in fact, there was no one at all. Knocking politely on the door inside a dark porch produced no results, so I hammered relentlessly until a French guest came down from her room upstairs and let me in. In the deserted reception area, I curled up uncomfortably in a chair, prepared to sleep there rather than venture out into the Malaysian night. Half an hour later the sound of a motorbike was followed by the appearance of a man who, with no more than a 'Come!', showed me to a room containing only a creaking bed and an ineffective fan. The communal washroom down the corridor reminded me of my turn-of-the- twentieth-century school changing rooms – plain bare tiles with a functional row of showers.

∞

The next morning, the female warden plied me with coffee and toast, apologising for the welcome, or lack of it. 'So sorry, dear. Very bad man. He's not allowed to leave the building at night. I will give him big punishment.'

Leaving her to plan the unfortunate night watchman's penance, I set out to explore KL. After a month of wondering where Kayelle was, I had finally twigged it was the common shorthand for Kuala Lumpur. I had an excellent street map torn out of the in-flight magazine, but any guilt at this act of vandalism had vanished when the man next to me on the plane carefully cleaned the metal cutlery provided with the meal before slipping it into his bag.

The map led me first to Chinatown – very different from Singapore – where a crowded maze of stalls, overflowing with everything from sequins to kitchen sinks, filled the paths between the more elegant but equally colourful Chinese shops and eating houses. Like a rugby ball emerging from a scrum, I dragged myself out of the crowded, noisy market to wander the city in search of temples.

First on my list was the Hindu Sri Mahamariamman Temple, difficult to find as it was tucked away in a side street and surrounded by a building site. Well worth the search, it was the most ornate temple I'd ever seen, with turquoise and blue stonework covered by hundreds of brightly coloured carvings of horses, gods, dancers and warriors. Then I followed the river to the Jamek Mosque, whose pink and cream minarets, set among palm trees, tapered elegantly amidst the surrounding skyscrapers. Finally, I walked a long way through the enervating heat to visit the Chinese temple of Khoon Yam, where red lanterns dangled from every surface.

Even after such a tiny sample, I was ready to applaud Malaysia for being a multi-racial, multi-faith society with a wealth of temples of all creeds.

In the afternoon I switched my attention to tall buildings. Email correspondents had all agreed that the view from the KL Tower was better than that from the more famous Petronas Towers, but I felt I had to look at the Petronas, one of the highest buildings in the world. The gleaming silver twin towers, with ribs of steel and glass spiralling upwards, were very impressive, ultra-modern but unmistakably Islamic, and beautiful in a stark way. Walking backwards to try to fit the whole building into a camera shot, I crashed into a wall and realised that it was impossible.

Every time I headed in the direction of the KL Tower it reappeared even further away, but I eventually tracked it down not long before it closed. Though the building is shorter than the Petronas, the viewing area is higher, more than 400 metres above the city. A high-speed lift catapulted me up the building like a reverse bungee jump, too fast even to leave my stomach behind.

Just as I walked into the circular glass room, a body in a bright yellow baby-grow dropped past the window. Alarmed, I rushed forward and looked down, relieved to see a colour-coordinated parachute opening below. I'd stumbled upon a skydiving exhibition, where the contest seemed to be about who could pull the cord closest to the ground. My challenge, and that of a young Malaysian lad next to me, was to try to catch on film that moment of free-fall past the window. On each attempt the body flashed by too quickly and, before long, the battery in my digital camera was flat. At least that meant I could tear my eyes away from falling bodies and take in the panoramic views over the city below, a mass of skyscrapers interspersed with ornate spires and domes.

∞

In Malaysia I met three women, each of whom had something to teach me in my quest to become an independent woman and traveller. The first was Feliz, a resident Englishwoman who contacted me through the website offering a bed. I accepted, bade farewell to the YWCA and took the long taxi ride out into the suburbs.

This was my first website invitation to stay with a total stranger and I was apprehensive lest she turn out to be an axe murderer or dotty recluse. In reality, Feliz was a dark-haired, fortyish bundle of energy who immediately put me at ease with the help of a few gins. Feliz had spoken with a clipped precision on the phone, but in the flesh she suffered from an extreme stutter. Unlike most people with this impediment, however, her speech deteriorated the more at ease she felt. After a few drinks, it took longer and longer for Feliz to tell me of her life sadly knocked off course by the death of her husband, Mike, six months earlier.

'What brought you to Malaysia?'

'Mike and I set up an advertising college about ten years ago. I lecture.'

Seeing my badly disguised surprise, she explained that when it came to public speaking, she didn't stutter. As a child, incomprehensible to peers and teachers alike, she was entrusted with one line in a school play. While the cast and staff alike sweated in apprehension as her part drew near, she knew it would be OK and the words came out faultlessly. Despite years of therapy, psychologists and the like, this remained the pattern of her speech.

'I never planned to go into advertising,' she laughed, 'but a man sitting opposite me on a train left a note behind when he got off, offering me a job.'

'What? Did you speak to him at all?'

'Not one word. It would have taken me the whole journey to say a sentence. I just turned up at the offices, was given a desk and there I sat until someone gave me something to do.'

Later, when her career in advertising had taken off, she met Mike in London when she was out for a drink with a colleague, and neither of them ever returned to their homes and spouses.

I wondered if it was pure fate or if certain people invite the extraordinary to happen. Both Feliz and I, for different reasons, were introverted children but had emerged in different ways, me by playing safe and retreating even further inward, Feliz by exuding confidence and taking risks.

Once divorced, I thought I was an independent, self-sufficient person and was only dimly aware that some colleagues and my children's friends seemed to find me rather scary. Over the past decade, I'd been gingerly letting down my defences and taking a few risks on the man front, surprised to find that the fun was worth a few knock-backs. This trip had felt like a chance to try out the new, more open Sue, and Feliz was an excellent role model.

∞

The next day, Feliz persuaded me to take a gigantic risk and go to a strange hairdresser. The humidity of Asia seemed to act like fertiliser and my hair was badly in need of a cut. Good hairdressers are like favourite baggy jumpers, comfortable, comforting and to be trusted, but I couldn't fly back to Ely just for Christopher to give me a trim.

The process began with a young girl giving me a shampoo. This wasn't the normal two minutes over the sink discussing holidays but a fifteen-minute scalp massage with long fingernails reinforced with superglue. At first it was enjoyable, the scalp tingling nicely, but after five minutes the fingernails became tridents and tingling became pain. Within the halo of fire emanating from my scorched head, the young Chinese male stylist got to work with the scissors. Hair fell on the floor at an alarming rate, as a trim turned into a major re-style that left me with very well cut but extremely short hair. At least I wouldn't have to worry about it again for a couple of months.

The hairdos were in honour of a concert that evening. I dragged out my one dress from the bottom of the bag and Feliz and I spent a 'Blue Peter' hour making Bruce a tuxedo and bow tie for the website. At the concert, a pleasant recital of accessible jazz, Feliz moved freely amongst the audience of expat intelligentsia and the young emerging artistic talent of Malaysia, introducing me as a journalist. At first embarrassed, I told myself to relax and be confident – what is writing on a website if not journalism? I was learning.

∞

After just two hours' sleep, I was up at 6am to catch the bus to Taman Negara National Park. I had enjoyed my stay with Feliz but was hungry for further experiences, and rainforest called. It was a measure of my newfound confidence, coupled with the realisation that expensive packages were unnecessary, that for most of my trip I merely turned up and bought a coach ticket.

Halfway along, we were transferred onto a flat-bottomed motorised canoe that chugged upriver, past bamboo villages with women washing clothes and men fishing from the bank. My second teacher, a gangly American woman sitting behind me, introduced herself: 'Hi, I'm Mary-Slater from Orlando, Florida.'

Like many women from the States, Mary-Slater had that confidence that allowed her to approach anybody and everybody and engage them in conversation. In her late thirties, she had an infectious enthusiasm for life and a wealth of experience of travelling as a single female. That evening at dinner on one of the floating restaurants that lined the river at the park HQ, I watched her in action as she drew an assorted collection of locals and visitors to our table to eat, drink and converse. I was full of admiration.

∞

We booked into a chalet together and the next morning set off into the rainforest. I was excited to walk in the jungle again – it felt like coming home. We chose a trail that took in the Canopy Walkway, a series of eight rope-walks suspended 25 metres above the forest floor, then the longest walkway in the world. It was some comfort to see that steel wires reinforced the ropes joining the wooden slats, but the bridges still swayed like playground swings. After I'd gingerly inched my way across the wobbling planks, Mary-Slater waited until the recommended 50 metre gap was between us before bounding across after me. Standing on the viewing platforms built round the gigantic trees that supported the walkways, we were level with the treetops, able to look deep into the jungle.

A boat trip down the river had been arranged with a young English couple we'd met the evening before but they failed to show up, traumatised, we heard later, by a nest of mice in their room. The boatmen were addicted to roaring up and down the river, revving their engines like demented chainsaws, and our driver went into a major sulk when Mary-Slater asked him to turn off the outboard motor and paddle us instead.

Floating down an offshoot of the main river, the dense jungle overhanging the water, no engine noise disturbed the sounds of the jungle: the hum of insects, chirruping of monkeys, and the hooting and squawking of the eagles, kingfishers and hornbills. Only Mary-Slater periodically broke the peace, excitedly shouting and pointing out a monitor lizard or an eagle. A keen environmentalist, she knew the names of most of the birds and animals, making me feel very ignorant.

Taman Negara was busier than the deserted Borneo parks but it was enjoyable to share the rainforest with Mary-Slater, who gave me lessons not only on wildlife but also how to shed layers of reserve when travelling alone.

∞

The rainforest was a tranquil haven, but twenty-four hours later I was back in KL, squashed among several hundred thousand Hindus at the Batu Caves. This was Thaipusam, described by the Lonely Planet as 'one of the most dramatic Hindu festivals (now banned in India), in which devotees honour Lord Subramaniam with acts of amazing masochism.'

Outside the caves, a tent city was littered with picnicking families and sleeping bodies, reminiscent of the outer ring of a pop festival. The path to the cave area was lined with stalls of garish Hindu icons, garlands and presents of limes and jugs of milk for the gods. Barbers, surrounded by mounds of black hair, worked furiously to shave the heads of men whose eyes glowed with a silent fervour as they queued patiently. The distant cacophony of drums and cymbals added to a growing sense of excitement and expectancy, and the pace quickened in unison.

Inside the festival area, the crowd gave off a yellow glow from saffron robes, golden flowers and lemon-coloured cradles containing babies granted in answer to prayers. Devotees in the central aisle, with the limes and jugs of milk attached to their bodies by hooks, their tongues and cheeks pierced by spikes and skewers, swayed and prayed as the procession inched forward.

But the spectacular vel kavadis dwarfed these painful acts of faith. The kavadis – huge metal cages with bright, tent-like covers decorated with neon holy pictures, flower sprays and an abundance of peacock feathers, rested on the carriers' shoulders, attached to the skin of their torsos by spokes and a multitude of hooks. The cries of 'Vel! Vel!' from the crowd, the drumbeats and chants of their band of supporters, drove them on in a trance-like state. It was a pulsating, gruesome, compelling kaleidoscope of colour and noise.

There was a solid mass of devotees in front of me climbing the 272 steps to the temple inside the Batu Caves. I was perfectly content to watch, taking in the sights and sounds until, miraculously in such a crowd, I bumped into Jit, a young student I'd met briefly at Feliz's house.

'You must climb to the temple,' he said. 'Come with me.'

'It's too hot, I'm quite happy here'

'You must do it for journalism,' he said cleverly, as he knew I now had no choice but to join the sweaty, heaving horde queuing at the bottom of the steps.

After half an hour I must have lost half my body moisture without even reaching the first step but suddenly there it was and the nightmare ascent began. Packed in among the faithful – men, women and even children – I picked my way slowly, step by step, through the carpet of discarded plastic water bottles, lost shoes and the occasional fainting pilgrim. The first-aid was well-organised and these unfortunates were whisked away. I soon lost Jit in the throng and, halfway up, was diverted into the middle lane by an official. This was where the kavadis were ascending and, though it wasn't so crowded and I could breathe again, I felt guilty to be in their midst as they plodded upward with their heavy loads, driven on by the drums, a few near exhaustion.

I reached the top on legs of jelly and entered the huge cave containing the temple. In contrast to the scene outside, the atmosphere in the cave was quiet and calm, the air refreshingly cool. The temple itself was suffused with an eerie glow formed by the shafts of light blazing down from the hole in the cave roof that merged with the fog of incense burning in braziers.

The devotees made their offerings and sat praying. The cave was so big that the huge crowd could spread out, granting breathing space and room to rest. There were niches with altars and statues of Hindu gods around the walls. Each niche had its own band of irreverent monkeys careering around at high speed or sitting on the heads of the statues. The peace was broken by a woman who, overcome by emotion, was screaming in a manic trance and had to be restrained by her followers.

When it was time to head back down, a bottleneck formed as pilgrims, spectators, devotees, helpers carrying the now-redundant kevadis and a hot, sweaty Netjetter tried to get through the narrow gap at the top of the steps. By now the heat and the crowds were beginning to make me feel claustrophobic and unwell, and I teetered on the edge of panic as people pushed from behind – there was nowhere to go. I refused to let my feet be lifted from the ground and, by the judicious use of elbows, managed to get safely through the gap.

Once on the steps, the crush eased and soon I was safely at the bottom. Exhausted and emotionally drained, I gulped down a huge Coke with ice, for once ignoring the health risk. Jit was lost forever and, needing to get away from people,

I caught a bus back to KL, numb from one of the most extraordinary mornings of my life.

Back in KL, it seemed the day had more excitement in store for me, as I stumbled upon a fortune-telling festival. At the time I was reading A Fortune-Teller Told Me by an Italian journalist, Tiziano Terzani. Warned by a fortune-teller not to fly for a year, the book recounts the author's year-long journey through Asia by alternative transport and his obsession with mystics and fortune-tellers. It's got to be fate, I thought – let's have a go.

MD Har Chao Wah was my seer. I chose her because she was a woman, the third to give me a personal insight on this leg of the trip. We encountered an early setback as I didn't know what time I was born, a crucial factor in drawing up my chart, but she struggled on womanfully and also read my palm.

'You are born in year of ox. You are metal, so lack water.'

'Does all that tell you anything about me?'

'Oh yes. It mean you give to others but do not ask or take for you. You also have problem keeping money.'

Mmm, the first bit was true until I abandoned my children to undertake this trip; the second was certainly true.

'Although you are creative, you lack energy.'

You'd be knackered too, if you'd had the morning I've had, I thought.

'The last three were not good years and you have been lonely. But best to come in your fifties. In seven years you will find love and prosperity.'

'Could it be sooner, please?' I asked, but she ignored me and carried on studying my palm.

'Your children give you trouble.'

A pretty safe statement to any parent.

'You could do with more weight. Your heart not good and trouble with breathing, so you must eat more fruit and vegetables, not meat.'

I'd lost about half a stone already on the trip and she'd seen me having a quick ciggie before going in.

'Gold and diamonds lucky jewels.'

The little jewellery I possess is all silver.

'You should try writing and will live into eighties.'

I liked that.

Well, not bad, I thought – probably over fifty per cent right. Good odds if you're observant. I could live with the instruction to eat properly, grateful that at least she didn't forbid me to fly.

This was the second time I'd had my fortune told. A friend at university, heavily into I Ching, had taken my reading; it prophesied that I 'would talk to the myriads of the people.' I've never forgotten those words and now, thirty years later, was I fulfilling my destiny with my weekly reports? Fanciful but interesting. What I would remember from this session was the promise of love seven years hence.

∞

The next day, weary from the cultish and the occult, crowds and cities, I felt the lure of the beach and decided to go to an island off the west coast, Pulau Pangkor. When I'd discussed with Feliz where to go in Malaysia, she'd been scornful of this idea.

'Are you on your honeymoon?' Surprised at the question, it dawned on me that all my emailers recommending the island had, in fact, been newlyweds. Undeterred, I still fancied sand and sea even if the sex would be missing. Perhaps I could return for that when I met my future love interest.

Six hours of bus and boat later, I was on the island in the little village of Teluk Nipah where, on the very edge of the forest, I settled into one of the ramshackle but 'simple' chalets. The jungle was on all sides and I sat on the veranda surrounded by exotic plants, listening to the insects and birds.

A voice from the chalet next door called over. 'Hello, we are from Norway. Remember to put a rock over the shower drainage hole and shut the bathroom door at night to keep out the rats.'

'Nice to meet you. Thanks, I'll do that,' I replied.

The plan to explore the island by bike was discarded in favour of my first sunbathe of the trip on a quiet stretch of beach. When I was broiled enough, I stepped into the wonderfully warm, blue sea. Always driven to see and do as much as possible, I'd forgotten that I was allowed to rest occasionally. The weekly reports to the Guardian were a factor, as it would be boring to write that I lay on a beach all week, but this was a once-in-a-lifetime chance and I was unlikely to return to these places. I didn't have the luxury of youth when there is always tomorrow. Carpe diem can leave you feeling pretty knackered if you carpe every diem for six months.

My ankles needed more oil and I was about to attend to them when the rain came down, and down, and down, and did so for the next twenty hours. Back at the chalet, I waved to my Norwegian neighbours, showing them my carefully chosen rock, plenty big enough to cover the hole, and settled down to sleep.

I'm not normally too bothered by the thought of creepy crawlies and had learned to ignore the soft pattering of the ever-present geckos on the walls and ceilings, but that night it was no gentle pitter-patter that woke me but the loud rasping of clawed feet on the wooden floor. I sat up in bed, the hairs on my neck as rigid as my body. With the rain still falling, there was neither moon nor stars to illuminate the black void surrounding me. When the rustling of the plastic bag containing my snack supply – deliberately left off the ground, on the table – augmented the noise from the floor, I choked back a scream. Were my unwelcome visitors about to attack? Was that an exploratory nibble or were my toes just trembling?

Cruelly, my torch failed and, after a desperate shaking and banging, I threw it down in disgust. The light switch was well beyond the end of the bed, impossible to reach without exposing a limb to attack. My only weapon was a very squeaky bed, and after throwing myself about like a child on a bouncy castle, while shouting 'la la la' at the top of my voice, I leapt across the room and switched on the light. My eyes were shut tight as I didn't want to see whatever it was that scampered away, probably as terrified as me. Leaving the light on all night, I dozed sitting up, woken frequently either by the torrential rain or scratching sounds on the roof. It was easily my worst night's sleep of the trip.

∞

The dawn was a relief, even though the rain was still falling, and I was happy about returning to KL that morning as my sister Maureen and her husband, Ray, were visiting Malaysia. Both retired and reaping the rewards of careful planning and good investment, they were the proud owners of three timeshares and used their 'points' to take several holidays a year all over the world. They'd been planning to go to Cuba but when I became a Netjetter they changed destination to meet me en route. After a week in Singapore they were travelling to KL and had offered me the spare room in their timeshare flat in a resort just outside the city.

A taxi ride later and there they were. We aren't a family of emotional extroverts but I was really pleased to see my sister and we had a rare hug. We are not very much alike, my sisters and I. All the other women in my family are short, inclined to roundness and graced with ample chests. I, however, am a throwback to some unknown ancestor – taller than my father and the thinnest and least well-endowed female in the clan. Thirty years later, my chest was still no match for my sister's, but I couldn't resist pointing out that, for the first time ever, I had the better suntan.

My first taste of timeshare accommodation impressed me, as it not only had a swimming pool, a pub and fancy restaurant, but also fluffy towels changed daily, tea and coffee whenever you wanted, air conditioning and a washing machine.

Feeling the seasoned traveller, I swaggered slightly as I showed Maureen and Ray round KL. In Chinatown, after sheltering from another tropical storm, a stallholder tipped up his tarpaulin to get rid of the rainwater as I walked by. Everyone, especially my sister, seemed to find it hysterical that I was soaked from head to foot. Beware the sin of pride.

∞

The next morning we headed up to the Cameron Highlands in another luxury – a hired car. After several hours driving along winding roads through forested hills to the little town of Tanah Rata in the Highlands, it was my turn to repay the compliment and introduce Maureen and Ray to budget accommodation at the 'basic but clean' Seah Meng Hotel. They took it very well, only commenting on the stringy, almost transparent towel and lack of coffee-making facilities.

The Cameron Highlands is a range of rolling hills covered with strips of tea-bush corduroy among the forested mountains. At a tea plantation we had a tour round the factory, seeing the whole process from leaf to packet. The one disappointment was to discover that the days of smiling saried tea pickers had gone and the new top leaves were now taken off with an electric strimmer.

On a walk through the forest, yet another storm broke. You could tell Maureen had been a Guide and Ray a Scout in their youth, as out came two umbrellas, under which we tried to shelter deep in the forest. The heavy rain soon seeped into all nooks and crannies and this time Maureen won the wet T-shirt competition.

Very muddy and damp, we made our way back to the hotel, cleaned up and ventured out to try the local dish, the 'steamboat'. A large tureen of hot, spicy water was placed in the middle of the table and a dish of raw bits of things, including an egg, was provided. There were recognisable vegetables like bean sprouts and kale, chunks of meat of some sort, and white and grey lumps that smelt fishy, but most of it was a mystery. We dropped bits into the water at leisure and, after guessing the cooking time, hooked them out. The noodly and vegetably bits were fine, but I couldn't eat the assorted fishy lumps, as the mere sight of slippery aquatic creatures turns my stomach.

∞

Next morning, poor Maureen, who had been ill in the night,

107

either from the soaking or the steamboat, looked very pale and exhausted. Ray took the hairpin bends very sedately to prevent unnecessary suffering. We were heading down the coast to see the fireflies at Selangor on our way back to KL. The rain was still falling relentlessly I'm sure I heard mumblings of 'Cuba' drift over from the front seats.

The long road to Selangor ran a couple of miles inland from the sea but there was no sign of resorts or tourist attractions so, curious, we took a side road towards the coast. At a little fishing port, we met the stares of the locals with a smile as we wandered around. This working port had that oily, scaly film that seems to cover the ground and permeate the air wherever there are boats and nets. Seeing the miles of grey mud and the narrow channels of water that constituted the coast, it became obvious why there was no tourism: step off the grass and you were likely to be swallowed up forever. The guidebook said that the fireflies didn't venture out in the rain (and who could blame them), so we abandoned the search and headed back to KL.

∞

The next day was our last together and my last in Malaysia so, as the sun was shining, we decided to seek fireflies once more, meandering at a leisurely pace and stopping wherever the fancy took us. After a visit to a park where tame monkeys took bread from our hands and to a nature reserve alive with sand flies – the one insect that adored my flesh and who feasted heavily – we arrived in Selangor just as the sun was setting.

As a beautifully clear night fell, we took a rowing boat up the Selangor River, so there was no engine to disturb the peace and quiet. To make up for the night before, the fireflies in the berenbang trees along the riverbank put on a fantastic show for us, with mile after mile of bushes aglow, twinkling like rows of Christmas trees. Our little boat glided through ripples of silver glitter created by the reflection of the fireflies and of the stars on the water. It isn't often my sister is lost for words but we all gazed in silent awe at the illuminations created by these tiny creatures.

'No fireflies in Cuba,' was my only comment.

So it was goodbye to family and to Malaysia, a wonderful place, and on to the last Asian stop – Bali.

7

Sarongs Are So Sexy

Bali had never appeared on my travel wish list, partly because I didn't know where it was but also because it had seemed too exotic for me, with my council estate background and public-sector credentials. I'd considered joining a tour for my ten days here, but Malaysia had given me such a boost of confidence that I thought I'd manage on my own. Arriving at 1am., I booked into a hotel in Kuta and didn't wake until midday.

'Am I too late for breakfast?' I asked the boy in reception, who laughed politely and directed me to the centre of town. Kuta, Bali's main resort, had a surfeit of shops selling wind chimes, wooden cats, hippie clothes and surfing gear, and the pavements overflowed with would-be guides, touts, tanned Antipodean surfers and sunburnt Europeans. After a late breakfast, I had a look at the beach, which was full of nubile, bikini-clad sun worshippers and male posers strutting with surfboards. I didn't much like Kuta, so caught the bus to Ubud.

Leafing through the guidebook for accommodation, the Dewi Putri Homestay attracted me as it was very cheap and belonged to a family of painters. Tucked away in a little lane, it took me a while to find as the entrance was obscured by flowering shrubs and trees. It was my first experience of Bali's extremely good-value losmen, guesthouses with small cottages or chalets in the verdant grounds of a family home. The cold shower and an inadequate fan posing as air-conditioning kept the cost down, but the family was welcoming and my room had a little porch that looked onto the lush garden and the large open-sided veranda where the family spent most of the day.

Far from my image of a Parisian garret lined with huge canvases and inhabited by a bohemian artist spattered with acrylics, the studio was a tidy office where the father, in a spotless sarong, showed me his collection of miniature, traditional rural scenes. His shy daughter hovered expectantly when he moved on to her bland attempts at watercolour washes.

In the chalet next door was an American, Ed, a fellow solo traveller about my age, who invited me along to a dance show that evening. Bruce seemed to wink, a difficult challenge with bead eyes. In a weird coincidence, Ed had a well-controlled stutter but he was a seasoned traveller and easy company.

'What do you do for a living that enables you to spend so much time travelling?' I asked after he'd reeled off all the countries he'd visited.

'Oh, a bit of this and that,' he answered evasively. 'I'm an entrepreneur.'

'And what are you currently entrepreneuring?'

'At the moment I have a business renting out storage space.'

I was rather disappointed, expecting a new invention or a business empire. Silly really, as no one in that league would be staying in a hut without air-con. Chatting about home, I told him about my three children and asked if he had any family.

'I don't seem to have much luck with women. In fact I've never actually lived with a woman. I better go now; I have to phone my mother. See you later.'

Famed as the cultural centre of Bali, Ubud contained an abundance of craft shops, cafés and little art galleries, and hosted a dance show most nights. Ed and I headed off to the Ubud Palace, former home of the rulers of Ubud but now a hotel, to watch a series of formal dances in bright, elaborate costumes and intricate headdresses. The beautiful girls in gold-and-red silk sarongs performing the Legong dance moved in intricately choreographed steps, their eyes fixed sideways in an unblinking stare and their expressive hands communicating in intricate sign language. Their feet never left the ground; in contrast, the handsome youths, with their sarongs hitched up, whirled about energetically in dances portraying manly warriors, kings and the eternal battle between good and evil.

The dancers were accompanied by the traditional music of Bali, a combination of bongs, clangs and jangles produced by an ensemble of gamelan, golden xylophones, gongs and strangely shaped stringed instruments. The colour and pageantry of the open-air show was set off by the elegant grounds of a courtyard guarded by statues of elephants and lions.

∞

A delicious breakfast appeared on the veranda in the morning: a dish of fruit followed by a pancake, with a big flask of tea. Ed joined me and I tagged along when he went to visit a couple he'd met in Ubud. James from New Zealand and Dominique from France were both in their thirties, with that laid-back, take-life-as-it-comes attitude of people who spend a lot of time on the road. With flowing black hair, Dominique was beautiful and oozed a confidence and sexiness unique to the French. James, in a silk sarong, was not only tall, tanned and handsome, but softly spoken, intelligent and witty, something close to my ideal man. I sighed inwardly and was lost in a fantasy of being twenty years younger, with Dominique carried off by a French smuggler to a remote chateau in Nepal, leaving James and me to ride off into the Bali sunset.

'Sue? Sue? Would you like to come in with us?'

'Mmm, yes please,' I answered, not knowing what I was agreeing to, but content it was James who'd asked. I had, in fact, agreed to share the hire of a car to go to the volcano at Batur. We drove through little villages, passing woodcarvers in their workshops and farmers toiling in the fields. The Balinese are an artistic and attractive people (everyone seemed to be able to paint, carve or dance), and they are also religious –

Baku National Park

Rainforest tree roots

Above: Mulu Airport

Left: Borneo Bearded Pig

Below: Taman Negara
National Park

Sri Mahamariam Temple

Thaipusam Festival – Batu Cave

Above: Kel Kavadis
Below: Sister and brother-in-law in
Cameron Highlands

Above: Ubud Dancers
Below: Bali paddy fields

Above: Bali Transport
Below: Melaga Mas Temple

Tana Lot Temple

Tirtaganga Singers

Hindus within predominately Muslim Indonesia. Each morning, women left canang, little offerings of grain, fruit and flowers on banana leaves, on every doorstep, nook and cranny to appease the gods and spirits. The dogs of Bali never went hungry.

Food preoccupied Ed and James, who'd developed a macho rivalry to see who could out-native the other. We stopped for a snack at a local roadside food stall, where Dominique and I declined the satay-with-flies and made do with a packet of biscuits while the men tucked in.

'Mmmm,' I said. 'Donkey intestine with salmonella confit.'

'Looks delicious,' said Ed, trying to get the satay to his mouth without an attendant bluebottle.

Avoiding the main roads and towns, we drove along quiet backstreets looking for a temple complex from Ed's Hidden Bali book. The site was deserted apart from the statues of gods and monsters who guarded the temples. We entered the complex clad in sarongs with appropriately coloured sashes, yellow for women and red for men. My collection of sarongs from the market in Ubud had been intended as presents but I ended up wearing them myself.

The temples rose before us, tall pagodas constructed from dark and sombre stone – very different to the gaudy Hindu temples of India, topped as they were with little thatched roofs and surrounded by lush, overgrown gardens. The atmosphere was serene and peaceful and we wandered happily for an hour, enjoying the quiet and space for reflection.

Serenity was in short supply at the village of Penelokan, lookout point for the steep Gunung Batur volcano. We had only five minutes to look at the giant mountain with its four craters before heavy cloud and a group of particularly aggressive and persistent vendors descended.

'Beautiful sarong, you buy. I give you special price,' screamed one woman, thrusting half a dozen sarongs into Dominique's hands.

'You buy bananas,' said another, grabbing my sleeve.

'Maybe later,' I replied, as we dived into a café to escape.

I realised my mistake when, ten minutes later, the same woman shouted at me through the doorway of the café. 'You! Lady! You promise buy bananas!'

She seemed oblivious to the fact that interrupting my lunch made me cross and unlikely to buy anything. With economic and political unrest throughout Indonesia, tourism was slow in Bali and the aggression was tinged with desperation.

To escape, we drove down a road that wound round the volcano close to Lake Batur and, stopping to admire the mountain amidst the tumbling black volcanic rock, congratulated ourselves on getting away from the sellers. The buzz of an engine broke the peace and a young man on a scooter materialised beside us, looking decidedly perplexed when the foreigners burst out laughing.

'Where in hell did he come from?' we exclaimed in unison.

'Sarongs?' guessed Dominique.

'Son of banana-lady?' I whispered.

'Hello, where you from?' asked man-on-scooter, looking slightly nervous. 'My father artist. You look at paintings?'

This drove us into further paroxysms of laughter.

'Very good paintings, I give you good price!' was his last-ditch effort.

By now he was obviously wondering which foreign asylum we'd escaped from and, while we wiped away tears of laughter, he drove off shaking his head. The return journey was undisturbed.

∞

Back at the losmen, my host not only continually reminded me of my promise to visit his gallery but also parked his new for-hire mountain bike outside my room every day. Patient persistence was finally rewarded when I hired it for an afternoon and set off with optimism but no itinerary.

After twenty minutes of wobbling unsteadily amidst the traffic of Ubud while the chain jumped erratically between the gear cogs, I was near the end of my endurance. Boiling hot and with a mouth full of dust, the sight of a roadside café proved irresistible. Having washed away the worst of the dust with a glass of watermelon juice, I looked up to discover that, fortuitously, I'd stopped right opposite the Neka Art Museum. Deciding my quota of galleries was rather low, I went in. After two of the four pavilions of traditional and modern Balinese work, I'd had enough of paintings. Museums and galleries rank with opera and olives: every five years or so I have an urge to try and persuade myself that I like them.

Returning on quiet hilly back roads, in danger of being propelled over the handlebars by the inconsistent brakes on the downward slopes and with my calves refusing to produce the necessary strength for the ups, I walked most of the way back. My reward was to wander along lanes where a foreign face still merited a stare, and I found a roadside café where nobody spoke English, an achievement in Bali today. This was what I really enjoyed doing: sitting outside a café people-watching.

∞

Ed hadn't appeared all that day and, when he failed to turn up at breakfast next morning, I knocked on his door. A grey, sweaty face covered in stubble appeared.

'S-s-something I ate, I suspect,' groaned Ed.

'Oh dear,' I replied. 'The harsh price of a non-native immune system.' As I gave him water, sweet tea and aspirin I hummed, 'There Was an Old Lady Who Swallowed a Fly.'

So I joined three English youngsters and a shy young Japanese couple – who continuously mopped their brows with little white towels – on a half-day 'sunset' tour of West Bali.

First stop was Alas Kedaton, the monkey forest, also home to a multitude of bats dangling from the trees like dark fruit. The monkeys here were the greediest, most badly behaved of animals. Rather than waiting to receive the nuts offered by the Japanese in exchange for a photo, they grabbed, bit and threatened until the terrified girl threw the whole bag at them and ran.

The monkeys stirred the forgotten memory of class 10T, a

group of nasty thugs who gave me hell in my first teaching job twenty years before. There had only been one ray of light in that dark year, when the aged parents of one dim pupil thanked me for his bottom grade in history – the only qualification he'd achieved.

After stops at the Pura Taman Ayun, a walled temple complex surrounded by a moat, and a batik shop, we moved on to Tanah Lot, site of one of Bali's sacred temples that guard the island from evil. Although visitors are not allowed inside, the cliff-top walk gave beautiful views of the temple, perched on a rocky outcrop and battered by rolling layers of foaming surf thundering in from the rough sea. As dusk fell, the cliff top sprouted whiskers as tripods were erected by earnest photographers who fiddled with light meters and lenses, their agitation increasing as the daylight faded. The transition between day and night was spectacular, with the dark outline of the rocks and pagoda roofs silhouetted against the varying pink and purple shades of the tropical sunset.

Back in Ubud, I collected up a languid but recovering Ed for a last meal with James and Dominique, as the next day they were all heading for Lovina in the north.

∞

After Ed had left, a very upset host arrived at my veranda, as Ed had left a 100 instead of a 1,000-rupiah note for his rent. I promised my host that I would look out for Ed during my travels round the island and ask him for the missing money.

'Thank you. I'm sure just mistake,' said the artist, dubiously.

It was time for me to be on the move as well, and I caught a bus for Tirtagangga, a quiet village with a water palace set among paddy fields, with views of the surrounding mountains, which had been recommended by an emailer as a good spot to relax. After booking into the Homestay Rijasa, which had a little restaurant and bar on the front and chalets behind in a beautiful garden, I wandered around the palace, a series of terraced pools, moats and fountains with statues of lions and monsters spitting out water. Locals were swimming in two of the pools but as they were all male I didn't want to risk a diplomatic incident by having a dip. I walked to the surrounding paddy fields, picking my way alongside gullies of water and soggy rows of young rice plants. Happily splashing through irrigation streams and negotiating stony paths, I only saw an occasional farmer hoeing on a distant terrace until I turned a corner to find a couple of women standing legs apart in the dyke. My best I'm-a-foreigner-but-I'm-friendly smile died on my lips when the rolled up sarongs and hostile glares alerted me to the business they were doing in the privacy of their own dyke. I hastily averted my eyes and hurried past.

The fields ended and turned into woods and only gradually did I realise that I had no idea where I was. Paths criss-crossed the woods and I followed what looked like the most-used route, but it merely ended at a T-junction of more paths. Intending to take only a short stroll, for once I had gone out without the guidebook. My mind was blank and I couldn't remember the name of the village. I knew it had a T and a G, but little else. Determined not to panic, I tried retracing my steps, but the proliferation of paths confused me even more and I couldn't even find the fields again, never mind the village.

Long live children! They are all angels blessed with the ability to communicate without the inhibiting need for language or social conventions. Standing in a glade scratching my head, two little boys appeared. Unfazed by a foreigner mumbling 'tergi, titiga, ganit, gonger,' they immediately grasped the problem and pointed down a path. Resisting the urge to kiss them, I hurried off in the direction they'd indicated.

Everything was fine until the path seemed to lead right through the courtyard of a rough hut – not in itself alarming, but the fierce-looking woman standing in front of it was. Arms folded, face hostile, she stared at me as if daring me to walk a step farther. I paused until the appearance of her even fiercer looking dog broke the impasse. With the mangy mongrel barking furiously and snapping at my heels, I resisted the urge to either burst into tears or run, and walked briskly across her courtyard and away through the trees until the dog gave up and returned to its surly owner.

By now exhausted and dehydrated, I was relieved to see the water gardens appear in front of me and rushed to the homestay, collapsed on one of the benches at the front and downed a large beer.

As my breath and equilibrium returned, I was joined by the other residents: Jon, a rugged eighteen-year-old Canadian backpacker (whom I'd liked to have met ten years before James), a female Japanese hippie woman (a rare phenomenon) and a young Japanese lad with orange hair (a very common phenomenon). The bar was also a magnet for the local young men, who acted as guides and did odd jobs for the homestay and its guests. So began the first of many hours spent chatting and lazing about with this group. We drank beer, swapped travel stories, ate, played cards, heard about life in Bali, described life in the rest of the world, played cards and drank beer.

In Tirtagangga, with no bus, train or plane to catch for a while, no must-do tourist sights, no internet, locals more than happy to spend time chatting, hot sun and plenty of cheap beer, I completely unwound for the first time since I'd set off over two months before. I sat with Bruce on my veranda in the balmy evening admiring the view over hills and rice terraces, the sound of frogs and cicadas filling the air.

'Mmm, I should do more of this relaxing, Bruce. I could get used to it.'

∞

After a day of rest I fancied a walk to another of the sacred temples that guard Bali, the Lempuyang Luhur, perched at the summit of Gunung Lempuyang, from which the guidebook promised 'the most staggering view over Bali.' A leader among the local lads named Made, who had appointed himself as my personal adviser and guide, immediately offered to drive me there. Presenting myself next morning, suitably saronged and sashed, I was momentarily taken aback by the transport arrangements: a shiny motorbike. Excited rather than daunted, I donned the helmet – little more than a tin hat – and off we went.

In Bali, as in Malaysia, the drivers of scooters and motorbikes customarily wear their jackets back-to-front so their chest is covered and the back bare. In the balmy air it couldn't be for warmth or protection from the rain, so I guessed it was to protect their clothes from splattered insects. Half an hour later, covered in a few dead creatures of my own, I was safely deposited at the base of the mountain with a promise I would be picked up in the afternoon.

It was the beginning of a week of festivities that led up to the Galungan, one of Bali's major festivals. The lower temple, Telaga Mas, was busy with a throng of Balinese building bamboo shelters with thatched roofs and assembling offerings of woven leaves and food. Having climbed the steep steps up to the shrine, I was just catching my breath when two white-suited officials positioned themselves either side of me, indicating that I must go back down. Had I unwittingly committed some cultural faux pas? Was my mere presence offensive? Only when they had frog-marched me to the bottom of the steps and stood there hand in hand did it become clear that they wanted me to take their photograph. At the first attempt, they weren't impressed by what they saw on the back screen of the digital camera and they marched back into position; and only when they were satisfied did they let me go on my way.

So, with an assortment of pilgrims – men in yellow sarongs, white shirts and headbands, women in all shades of silk and lace – I began the two-hour climb up the steps to the upper temple at the mountaintop. Men carrying 20-foot bamboo poles, women with heavy baskets of fruit on their heads and boys taking fresh stocks of bottled water to the sellers stationed en route passed by me, the only communication being by smile or gesture. During rests, I looked out over miles of terraced paddy fields and wooded valleys, with Gunung Agung, Bali's biggest volcano, in the distance. Near the top, we entered a white cloud so I wasn't able to enjoy the view from the simple temple at the summit.

Back at the lower temple, I was the object of much benign curiosity, and was invited to sit with the youngsters making offerings. As both sexes here wear sarongs and the women, without exception, have very long, thick black hair, one young man was obviously unsure as to whether I was a man or woman. I was consoled by the laughter of the others and his embarrassed sign language indicating that my hair, still very short from the Malaysian shearing, had confused him. Despite my poor showing as both a photographer and a woman, I enjoyed being the sole foreigner accompanying the ordinary Balinese on this journey. For once, I hadn't felt like an intruder or voyeur but a welcome guest.

The lovely day was not yet over, as every Sunday evening the men of the village put on a show for visitors in an open-sided hall at the back of my homestay. Far from the polished, professional shows of Ubud, this comprised fifteen bare-chested men and boys playing a few instruments, dancing and singing local songs in a Balinese rap accompanied by hand- and finger-waving. Goodness, they were a handsome lot, with beautiful, clear, hairless skin, rippling muscles and big, wide smiles. As the local firewater was passed around the songs became louder and more raucous, and members of the audience were persuaded to join the dance.

Either it was the influence of all this vibrant youth or something in the Bali air, but I seemed to fancy every male on the island with the exception of Ed who, unfortunately, was the only one who might have been interested. After the show the drinking carried on late into the night but, by now feeling old, tired and a little sad, I retired early to my big, empty bed.

∞

A good walk was what I needed. Not wanting to make the same mistake twice, I engaged Made as my guide, not only through the paddy fields but to life on the island. We chatted as we walked through and over paddy fields with their trenches of water.

'All people own land, me too, but I don't want to be a farmer.'

'What do you want to do?'

'I want to work for tourists. I will get good transport for them.'

'Are you saving your money?' I asked, thinking that he had already had a sizeable sum out of me.

'No,' he said, looking abashed. 'After I give some money to my mother, I go to cockfight.'

'You spend it all there? How often are the cockfights?'

'Every day,' he replied wistfully.

The sound of crowing from every direction announces Balinese mornings, and cockfighting is a national obsession. Women aren't allowed in but Jon, who'd been to a fight, said that he'd been taken aback by the savagery of it, with long talons being fitted onto the claws of the cocks. Mercifully the contests were short.

Made took me to his village, where the huts in the family compound were of the traditional wood and mud, with no electricity or running water. An old lady showed me her kitchen, crammed with stored provisions, cooking implements and an open fire. Next door, a young woman and her toddler were fascinated by the digital camera and were more than happy to have their photo taken.

I sensed no envy or resentment amongst these young Balinese, just an insatiable curiosity about the rest of the world. The nearest internet café was three miles away but the lads all made frequent trips and were keen to receive email messages. Here, as in Malaysia, people were used to young student backpackers and rich people in big hotels, but an older woman backpacking on her own puzzled them.

It wasn't long before Made asked the inevitable question. 'Where is your husband?'

'I'm divorced,' I replied, deciding to be truthful.

'Oh, so sorry, so sorry.' Made was overcome with confusion.

'It's OK. My ex-husband and I are still friends.' He

obviously found this difficult to take in. 'Do people get divorced in Bali?'

'No, never. I don't want to get married. I like to be with tourists.'

While we were walking a pack of dogs appeared and followed us, barking furiously, and I glimpsed a man watching us from a hill, taking a close interest in our progress. Made took my arm and we quickly walked on until we were past the danger.

'Many dogs in Bali – to protect property,' he said.

'Would they have attacked if you hadn't been with me?' I asked nervously, remembering my solo walk a few days earlier.

'Maybe,' replied Made, as we stopped at a dyke. 'You want swim?'

Having previously witnessed one dyke's uses, and considering the fact that we were standing next to a man washing his cow in the water, I declined.

That afternoon I left my little haven and headed north to Lovina for a bit of beach before I left Bali, catching the local bus, which had a scattering of backpackers including an American girl, Jessica, travelling on her own. Now an expert on travellers' body language, I could recognise the rigid concentration on her book as a defensive ploy to avoid looking lonely. After engaging her in conversation, we dined in a restaurant on the beach and I told Jessica my plan to spend a couple of days here, head back to Ubud on Wednesday to pick up my big bag, fly Thursday evening and land in Darwin on Friday 1st.

'I think you'll find that the 1st is Thursday. Also, Wednesday is the big festival, a public holiday with no buses running.'

I was thunderstruck. Somewhere I'd managed to lose two days, so there was nothing for it but to head back to Ubud in the morning and forgo the planned couple of beach days.

∞

Luckily there was just time for a dawn trip to go dolphin-watching. At 5.30am I was perched in one of the little group of catamarans that set off from the beach, the buzzing of the engines disturbing the peace of the early morning. A half-hour into the ocean, we positioned ourselves to wait, watching the rising sun send showers of sparkles across the water. When two black dots that I assumed were dolphins were spotted far in the distance, we appeared to head back; that was it, I thought cynically, the dark specks ensured that they didn't have to give us our money back. But I was wrong and we sped towards a group of a dozen dolphins in the distance.

A crazy chase followed, the dolphins surfacing in majestic leaps, disappearing, reappearing in another direction while we careered around, eyes peeled to spot the sleek grey beasts, who seemed to enjoy taunting the cumbersome boats. My task was to capture a photo, which was difficult as neither the boat nor the dolphins would stay still. As if putting on an exhibition for our benefit, the pod grew to twenty, with several extroverts pirouetting on the surface, while the others leapt in unison. After an hour, tired of the game, the dolphins headed out to sea, leaving me exhilarated and grateful that, despite my disorganisation, I'd been able to see their show.

Then it was straight onto the bus for the long ride back to Ubud, a picturesque journey as the whole island had been busily preparing for the Galungan festival, celebrating the triumph of good over evil. All the streets were adorned with penjor, long bamboo poles decorated with flags and with little offerings left at the base, while huge dishes of fruit were being arranged for the family temples.

Back at Dewi Putri, my host family was very busy. On festival day they dressed up in their finest sarongs and invited me to see the family temple tucked away in a corner of the courtyard. A blue and silver cloth covered the altar, which was piled high with large and small trays of offerings. Every pole, the thatched roof and the ceremonial parasol with a long yellow fringe was decorated with green and yellow silk and red ribbon, enough to tempt any god to visit.

The owner was so anxious about whether I'd seen Ed that I felt sorry for him, pretended that I had and gave him the missing money. After a hard bout of bargaining I also bought the painting that I'd fancied on the day I arrived. Considerably richer since my return, he set about sawing a piece of plywood to pack it flat.

Leaving this wonderful island and its beautiful, peaceful people to their festivities, I reluctantly prepared to move on to a new continent. My Asian adventure – always challenging, occasionally frightening but never dull – was over.

Waiting in the airport, I felt proud of myself. I recognised how far I'd come from the woman who sat trembling in her Mumbai hotel room. Only a couple of months had passed but in terms of experiences and emotions, it felt like a lifetime. Having survived Asia, I was tempted to think that Australia and New Zealand would be a doddle.

8

Toured Out

'Well Bruce, what do you fancy doing?' I asked as we stepped off the plane at Darwin, on the north coast of Australia. 'Surfing, sheep shearing or crocodile hunting?'

What immediately struck me about Darwin was the smell, reminiscent of changing rooms after a rugby tournament, which followed us to the luxurious YHA. With a smart reception area, swimming pool and laundry room, this was a long way from the barrack bunks, cold showers and compulsory chores of my teenage hostelling days, but one sniff of the room and my stomach heaved.

'Please, please can I change my room for one that doesn't smell?' I begged the young girl on reception.

'Sorry, mate. It's the rainy season. Everything stinks.'

Apart from its odour problem, Darwin was a quiet city, welcome after the hurly-burly of Asia. Clean and spacious, it had wide, empty boulevards and pedestrianised shopping precincts. Everyone wore shorts and sandals, making it impossible to spot fellow travellers. As it was quite flat, I risked another hire bike to explore the coast, a long sandy beach peppered with rocks but curiously devoid of people. So much for the Aussie legend of endless beach parties, I thought, as I clunked my way along, not a bikini or surfboard in sight.

After peddling for another couple of miles, I stopped for a paddle in the empty sea. Standing up to my ankles in the cool surf, I was close enough to read one of the notices.

With a high-pitched squeal, unbecoming of a mature woman, I leapt out of the water. Had my feet already been assaulted? After rubbing each toe to ensure there were no attachments, I pedalled furiously away from the water. Hot, flustered and breathless, my flight led me to a marina where I stopped for a beer.

Smiling amiably, I made my way to the bar, weaving through the yachting set at lunch – men in blue blazers and women with shoulder pads and high heels who, after one glance in my direction, stuck their noses either in the air or into their food. Maybe it was the hire bike or the scruffy shorts, or possibly the heavily scabbed knees still with traces of purple iodine from a fall in Bali, or my red blotchy feet that made them all sit as far away as possible. Whatever the reason, I drank my lonely beer and headed back to the hostel.

It was time to think about how and where to spend my four weeks in this vast land. As I had a flight booked from Alice Springs in the centre of Australia to Cairns on the East Coast, south through the outback to Alice was the obvious route. There seemed to be three options: firstly I could fly, but it was a costly way to see nothing but clouds; secondly, I could answer one of the ads for companions to share camper vans, but the person-specifications seemed to include limitless time and libido, both of which had to be carefully rationed by a fifty-one year-old whizzing round the world; the third option was to join the 'Oz Experience' – a backpacker's ticket that enabled you to jump on and off the buses that roamed Australia. This mode of transport had the affectionate nickname of 'The F**k Bus', and from my experience of backpacker hostels, I suspect it was well-earned. It might have livened up my reports if I'd opted for one of these last two, but to endure the sound of yet more student love-making through flimsy hostel walls would have been too painful.

I wanted to visit the rainforest in Kakadu National Park before leaving the Northern Territory. A blinding flash of capitalist inspiration struck me when I was in the tour agent's office: could my Guardian connection secure a discount for the three-day, four-wheel-drive trip to Kakadu in return for publicity on the website? Only someone from the public sector would have neglected to try this for so long.

'No problem,' answered the boss. 'Twenty-five per cent off, OK?'

'No problem,' I replied and, excited by this power, extended the deal to include a seven-day trip down to Alice Springs. The next two weeks were sorted.

∞

My twelve companions arrived at 6am the next morning: first, a Scandinavian female boxer built like Mike Tyson, followed by giggly Irish twins with boyfriends in tow, six multinational teenagers and finally a Danish couple in their sixties – for once, I wasn't the oldest. The Danes apart, these youngsters were a different sort from those I'd met so far; they were still mostly gap-year students, but they'd confined their year off to working and partying their way round Australia. Not for them the sturdy walking boots and canvas sun hats; they managed perfectly well with flip-flops, shorts, bikini tops and designer sunglasses.

Last to arrive was Andy, the tour leader, a young Paul Hogan in full bush gear, with a reputation for teasing snakes. Andy had an uncanny ability to drive and spot six-inch lizards in the undergrowth, wading birds with strangely-coloured legs or dingos lurking in the long grass at a distance of 500 metres. On one occasion we screeched to a halt to look at a ten-foot-long olive python which, true to his reputation, Andy teased with a long stick. We were shown assorted piles of insect dung, including impressively tall ones called cathedral termite mounds, and groups of thin slabs of it facing in the same direction known as magnetic termite mounds.

The highlight of the day was a trip watching crocodiles on the Adelaide River. As it was the rainy season, the crocodiles didn't spend their day lazing on the river bank so, to satisfy the tourists and to stop the crocs invading inhabited parts of the river, the rangers fed them a daily ration of three lumps of meat hung from fishing lines. As we cruised down the river, two big monsters jumped for their lunch, a spectacular sight as the great jaws snapped round a large chunk of cow. When, with breath-taking speed and accuracy, a large sea eagle swept down from the sky and whisked away the third piece, the warden generously decided that it wouldn't count, and hung out another. When Croc No 3 appeared, I went below to capture a close-up action shot of the gaping mouth. 'What a poser,' I thought, as the bulbous eyes bobbing in the water seemed to be fixated on the camera rather than the meat.

'Get that arm in!' the warden bellowed, and I took a picture of the empty sky as I hastily withdrew my juicy elbow, which had been hanging out of the window. The croc immediately lost interest in me and snapped up the meat. I wondered if my travel insurance would have covered provision of a limb for a crocodile's lunch.

On this expedition, I broke my vow never to sleep under canvas again. Bringing up children had involved a lot of camping, in particular the annual week at Waxham on the Norfolk coast, which involved a group of families camping in a field surrounded by sand dunes. With the passage of time, it was the children who sneaked off to the dunes to drink, the games were dismissed as childish and it became impossible to cope with the complicated relationships within reconstituted families, so the tradition petered out. Here on the edge of Kakadu, I was pleasantly surprised to see wallabies hopping around ready-erected, box-like tents – decidedly bearable. Meals on the trip involved everyone mucking in but there was always a noticeable absence of males when it came to kitchen chores.

Waiting for us and for the rain to stop were two Aboriginal guides: Kevin, a colonial throwback resplendent in dazzling white shorts, shirt and knee-high socks, and Ricky, in jeans and T-shirt. The duo had travelled the world demonstrating and promoting Aboriginal culture and were happy to answer our many questions about the Aborigine way of life.

'Do Aborigines marry?' asked one of the twins.

'Yes, but kinship rules are complicated and we don't have to stick to one partner.'

'You can have as many as you like?' chipped in an impressed Swedish lad.

'Yes, in some tribes.'

'Does that apply to both men and women?' I asked, ready to fight the female corner.

'Certainly,' said Ricky, knocking me out first punch.

The return of the sun halted our inquisition, and we all had a go at using a woomera, an Aboriginal throwing spear. Mine flopped out of the end of its launch-stick a couple of feet in front, and the rest of the group did little better, in contrast to Ricky's Olympic-length throw.

On a bush walk, we were shown the trees and plants that provide the food, moisture, medicine and fuel used to survive in the outback. Standing a couple of hundred yards away, Kevin demonstrated the Aborigine answer to the mobile phone, using hand and arm sign language to tell Ricky that it was time to come home for his tea.

In the evening, Ricky and Kevin discarded the Western clothes, donned paint mixed from water and crushed rock, and gave us a display of Aboriginal music and dance. I heard the didgeridoo, which I now knew was made from woolybark or stringybark trees, as never before as Ricky produced a wonderful array of sounds, including bird calls. The only low point was discovering that my damp rock seat was the home of several leeches, which dined on my thigh.

∞

The next morning we drove into Kakadu itself. It was the wet season so some parts of the park were closed but the rest featured lush vegetation: part savanna, with tall grass and taller eucalyptus trees, and part forest, with sheer limestone escarpments peppered with spectacular waterfalls crashing into rock pools. These provided natural swimming holes, perfect to cool off in after hiking in the sticky thirty-plus-degree heat. (We were assured that they were regularly swept for crocodiles.) I'd never sat under a waterfall before, or had a picture of myself in a bikini published on a website, nor been thrown out of my seat as a 4x4 rock-'n'-rolled over rough terrain and flooded roads. So many firsts in such a short time.

On the second day in the park we walked around Nourlangie Rock to see rock art. They were a scary lot, these figures painted onto the wall of a cave. The biggest was Namondjok, a Creation Ancestor who now lives in the sky and appears as a dark spot in the Milky Way. Beside him was Namarrgon, the Lightning Man, who uses the axes on his head, elbows and feet to split the dark clouds and create lightning and thunder. To the left was Nabulwinjbulwinj, a dangerous spirit who eats females after killing them with the strangest of clubs, the normally inoffensive yam.

This rainforest was interesting but very different from Borneo; for me, it was more a dalliance than a passionate affair.

∞

Back in Darwin, I barely had time to recover from the effect of all this youthful energy, not to mention the end-of-tour party – a raucous affair involving limitless jugs of beer, inter-tour rivalry and loud singing – before it was time for tour No 2. This time there were no Danish pensioners to mitigate the relentless youth of the other twenty-three passengers. Our leader was Meatloaf, so called on account of his tubby figure, ponytail and love of heavy metal.

With 1,500kms to cover in three days I had to get a real taste of Australia, even if it was only from the dust of the Stuart Highway, the long road that links Darwin to Alice Springs. The first 400kms to the town of Katherine, just down the road in Australian terms, was through savannah woodland, the air warm and muggy and carrying a whiff of Darwin. Katherine had only just reopened after severe flooding, and was crowded with Aborigines brought in from their water-logged homelands. Our band of international travellers terrified one little toddler, who froze and had to be picked up by his father before he dared pass us.

The boat trip down Katherine Gorge took us through two of the thirteen gorges where the wide river had forced its way through rugged steep rock, over rapids and down falls. After a swim, a walk and a visit to another rock art site it started to rain, and the boat crew abandoned us at the jetty. There was no sign of our bus. The rain was more like scaffold poles than stair rods, and the river rose before our very eyes.

As we huddled under the narrow eaves of a locked shed, someone discovered a box of bin liners and the humble black bag was transformed into rainwear. There was the black condom look, the casually ripped style with apertures for limbs, nose or head, while a few were pulled over both body and backpack in Quasimodo fashion. I'd forgone the mac in favour of fisherman's waders to prevent my walking boots, which had been robbed of their proofing by Steven's overzealous housemaid in Sarawak, taking in yet more water.

When the cold, wet procession had clambered back onto the bus, Meatloaf sang 'Bat out of Hell'. The campsite that evening was a scarecrows' convention, every pole and bush sporting a dripping article of clothing.

∞

One of the good things about these tours was that there was seldom any need to wash as we spent so much time in water. One-hundred kilometres from Katherine, there was another opportunity to swim in the Mataranka thermal pools, lakes at a constant thirty-three degrees surrounded by rich rainforest and palm trees.

As the temperature rose and we passed from the tropical Top End of Australia into the arid Red Centre, the scenery began to change, with trees thinning out, the spear grass getting shorter and scrubbier and the soil turning redder. Hour after hour we sped through the bare, flat land that stretched to the horizon, the highway snaking ahead like a red vein with only an occasional 'road-train' – lorries pulling five or six containers carrying the necessities of life from Darwin to Alice. The outback was huge and achingly empty, more desolate than I'd imagined. It was alluring yet somehow frightening, especially when Meatloaf regaled us with gruesome tales of people dying after leaving their broken-down vehicles.

Stops along the way were few and centred on pubs. First was Larrimah, at the end of the line where the first attempt to build a railway to Darwin had stopped. Next was Daly Waters, reputedly the oldest pub in northern Australia, which resembled a Wild West saloon, complete with a tethering pole for your horse. There was a smattering of locals in these two pubs, Australians in leather hats and khaki shirts, propping up the bar. They were friendly enough with the odd 'G'day', but reminded me of the farm labourers of the Fens, where living and working in isolated, far-flung communities engenders a suspicion of outsiders. I began to wonder if 'G'day' and 'No worries' were going to be the only words I would ever exchange with any Australians who weren't tour leaders or guides. So far I had not touched the lives of the convict descendants of my ancestors.

Our stop for the night, 664 kilometres from Katherine, was at Juno Horse Farm, built during Australia's last gold rush just outside the town of Tennant Creek. We were to sleep outside under the starry sky in swag bags, waterproof canvas sleeping bags complete with mattress, first used by migrant workers who travelled the land in search of work. We were all up for it but, as the light faded, the mosquitoes came out in even greater numbers than the stars. In winter being cocooned inside a swag bag would have been like returning to the womb, but on this summer evening zipping out the mozzies was to risk drowning in your own sweat. Although the little beasts don't find me tasty, the buzzing, slapping, squelching and swearing of the others ruled out sleep. One by one, accompanied by many expletives, the swag bags were rolled up and taken inside, leaving only me and four other hardy heroes to meet the dawn al fresco.

∞

Our journey continued across kilometre after kilometre of arid land, featuring little more than dirt and spindly shrubs. We were now well into the Red Centre of Australia, aptly named after its red rocks of unusual shapes and sizes. Our first dose was Devil's Marbles, filled with huge sandstone rocks eroded into clusters of round boulders, some perched precariously on top of others. Whoever named the place was spot on, as it did look as if the rocks had been carelessly tossed around by bored giants. The area is crossed by Aborigine dreaming trails, places where legends are passed down the generations.

The belief that the stones are the fossilised eggs of the Rainbow Serpent was much more romantic than any geologist's claim of erosion. The abandoned balls seemed incongruous in the silent and flat landscape and I felt shivers down my spine as I clambered round them.

∞

My early departure from the party the night before at Alice Springs meant I was the only one with a clear head – and an intolerance of the singing from the still-drunk Irish contingent – on the bus the next day. I was having an 'old' moment, when I longed for company of those from my own era, someone else who remembered Jimi Hendrix or Bob Marley when they were alive.

What surprised me about my age was that I seemed to have become a role model for middle-aged female Guardian readers. Though the newspaper printed only a small selection of emails on its website, I made a point of reading all that had been sent and answering as many as I could. I felt that if people had bothered to write, they deserved a personal response, even if it was only a line or two. Many of the emails came from women of a certain age who were either travelling themselves or were travelling vicariously with me. Some, emboldened by the fact that I hadn't broken any bones or been sold into slavery, were considering journeys of their own. I loved the idea of others like me setting off into the unknown, but there were many occasions when I wished I could bump into one.

Reading a few messages was a good antidote to feeling lonely but this, together with writing the weekly report, meant I spent an awful lot of time and money in internet cafés.

We explored the King's Canyon, an area of high red cliffs and gorges and camped in the evening among the rocks with a roaring fire. This was another swag-bag night, but the appearance of a scorpion chased many people into their tents or onto the bus, where they spent the night roasting slowly. There were no mozzies in this area and I spent a blissfully cool night in my swag bag staring at the blanket of stars before drifting contentedly off to sleep.

∞

My favourite hike of this tour was through the peaceful Kata Tjuta, commonly known as the Olgas, an expanse of massive red rocks overlapping and tumbling down to form valleys. The trail wound round these high, smooth, rounded domes that looked like a collection of bald heads and I enjoyed the peaceful atmosphere and a breeze that took the edge off the blistering heat.

As the afternoon wore on, we made our way to the most famous of red rocks, Uluru or Ayers Rock, to join hundreds of coaches taking up position for sunset. The red, whale-like rock, solitary in the flat scrubland, was huge and imposing but disappointing. I don't know if it was the hundreds of tourists, my mood or the familiarity of the scene, but I didn't share the excitement of the crowd. The cloud had disappeared, there was a beautiful pink sunset that turned the rock many hues of orange and red as the brochures promised, but I would have rather stayed in the quiet Olgas than join this circus.

Dawn saw us, and all the buses, back on the opposite side of the rock. The usual debate had been raging among my fellow tourists about the rights and wrongs of climbing the rock; although most were prepared to heed the Aborigine request not to climb it, a few saw it as their absolute right. Any argument became irrelevant as the climb was closed due to the wind, so we all walked the ten kilometres around the base.

Our leader said it would take us about three hours, during which time he was going to catch up on his sleep and have cake ready for our return.

Rock done in ninety minutes and cake eaten in five, we stopped at an artists' commune where Aborigine artwork was produced and sold on site. I bought a painting by a local woman artist, convinced of its authenticity by a hair stuck to the back.

Back at Alice Springs, after another end-of-tour party, it was time to say goodbye to my boisterous companions.

∞

I exchanged red rock for coral with the move from the frontier town of Alice Springs to tourist boomtown Cairns, a spacious city with clean, wide streets, numerous backpacker hostels and diving schools. Keen to see the ocean and the Great Barrier Reef, I booked a day on the Free Spirit, a yacht that ran trips with snorkelling, lunch and an optional introductory scuba dive. Initially intending only to relax in the sun as the boat sailed through turquoise water, I did have a go at snorkelling but the buoyancy vest confined the experience to a few blue fish near the surface. I can swim but I am not comfortable in water and hate submerging my head. As a small child paddling in the sea in Sussex, I once stepped out of my depth off a hidden shelf. All these years later, I can still remember that feeling of panic as I went under.

'Can we have numbers for the scuba dive?' asked the captain.

Bruce, out of the bag for some sun, seemed to give me a look that defied me to miss this opportunity and in a moment of madness my arm went up.

'OK, you're Number 6.'

I joined the sessions on safety and breathing in a daze. It didn't take long for the captain to note that arm Number 6 was attached to a quivering mass of abject fear and, while the others were allocated to groups, I had an instructor all to myself. As I grappled with the gear, my foreboding grew.

The weight of the tank pulled so hard on my shoulders that it was impossible to stand upright, and I couldn't walk in the ridiculously long flippers. Once the face mask was added, the rubbery smell added nausea to the list of woes.

'Do people really do this for pleasure?' I asked my tanned instructor but I don't think he heard me through the mask, which had steamed up.

Rather than jump into the sea like the intrepid youngsters, I lowered myself in gently, like a battered cod going into the deep fryer. My instructor allowed me only a few minutes to play on the surface before he took my hand and led me head-first deeper and deeper into the ocean. Terror outweighed exhilaration until we reached the reef and the colour and wonder dispelled the panic. I gave my instructor the OK sign that we'd practised on board.

Flat fish, fat fish, gold and silver fish, metallic blue, bright yellow, stripy, dotted and triangular fish wove around me in a dizzying swirl. Spiky, nobbly coral lay beside delicate sponges, waving multi-coloured seaweed and fat-fingered anemones that hid when we approached. The intensity of movement and colour was fit for a Disney cartoon. But this was deep in the ocean and the worries tumbled back into my head:

Suck or blow?

Leg cramp?

How to breathe?

Mask slipping?

Staying down became unbearable and I frantically signalled that I needed to return to the surface. When boat, sky and sun were visible again, I wrenched off the mask and gulped in lungfuls of fresh air, pretending not to notice my instructor flexing the hand that I'd been gripping.

After an inelegant return to the deck and the removal of the cumbersome tanks, I was overwhelmed by relief and elation. The experience had been so beautiful, so terrifying, so unlike anything I'd seen before, so awesome and so bloody awful that, not knowing whether to laugh or cry, I did both.

∞

To come down from the high of the dive and to get out of the sun, I hired a car and headed up the coast towards the Daintree Rainforest. The natives drove on the left and there wasn't much traffic, so I relaxed and enjoyed the freedom of the road until jungle lured me into the national park.

On a long, deserted stretch of coast, where the mangrove trees came right down to the beach, I abandoned the car and tramped through the swamp, fascinated by the weirdly shaped roots and trees rising from the water. On the empty beach, a dot appeared in the far distance and made a determined beeline in my direction. Was this the man of my dreams come at last to add sex to sand and sea? No, it was a woman, who politely asked me to take her picture beside the reef with the forested hills in the background and, when it was done, headed off in a different direction.

The long, solitary walk purged the stress of noisy tour buses and Cairns gave my batteries a much-needed recharge. The seven nights at Rosie's Backpackers was the longest at one establishment since leaving home, although my roommates changed constantly, with one set of giggly young English girls replaced by another.

∞

I'd tasted Australia's diversity – forest, outback, red rock and reef – and it was now time for some city life, so I flew to Sydney. I'd met Annie in Kathmandu before she set off with Carol's tour in India, and she'd invited me to stay when I reached Australia.

The only Australians I'd met in nearly four weeks were Peter and Sally, a couple I'd spent time with in the café in Bako rainforest in Sarawak, who invited me to dinner in Cairns. Two delightful days with website contacts Simon and Yuki, who lived on the coast north of Sydney, didn't really count as Simon was English and Yuki Japanese.

Annie, a thirty-something, well-travelled Sydneysider, took me for a quick tour of the city, which shared many of the London street names and districts. There all similarity ended, as Sydney was newer, cleaner, sunnier, more spacious, less stressed and had beaches.

The next day she drove me up to the Blue Mountains, a high range of sheer cliffs and walled canyons, not crossed by explorers until 1813. The name reflects the blue tinge produced by the abundant eucalyptus trees, but the Grey Mountains would have been more apt that day as the drizzly, misty rain didn't stop.

Annie generously gave me a key to her flat so I could come and go as I pleased while I explored Sydney. On a boat trip under the famous bridge by the Opera House, I jumped off at Taronga Zoo as I couldn't leave Australia without seeing a koala and an emu. After a field containing two angry emus that looked ready to spit at me, I spotted the koala pen but decided that a queue of excited children and adoring parents with big cameras stretched round the block wasn't worth it.

I'd been surprised that Australia's famous surfing beaches, including the unremarkable Bondi Beach, were actually in the city. After walking for miles along the coast, I stopped on a cliff for a rest and an ice-cream, looking down on that unique breed of beach life: surfers at play. To gain some understanding of this watery sport, I followed the progress of a blond, tanned Adonis in a bright red wetsuit who was easy to keep track of from my lofty look-out. Surfboard tucked under his arm, he ran into the waves, ducking under the surf for the long swim on the board out beyond the breakers. No more than a red dot, he rose and fell, rhythmically in tune with the sea, patiently waiting for the right wave. As it approached, there was a quickening of pace as he launched the board and scrambled onto it. My excitement rose ... but no, it was too soon; he fell off in a tangle of arms and legs and the wave passed by to crash, un-surfed, onto the beach. Another session of gentle bobbing then, standing upright, he caught the wave and rode it magnificently, and – yes! – in a climax of crashing surf, he landed right on the beach. The strong young red devil scarcely paused before heading back out to sea.

Would I add surfing to my growing list of accomplishments?

If it wasn't for all that head-under-water stuff, I might well have considered it.

∞

I dipped into the reports of my fellow Netjetters, Milly and Sam, and discovered that I'd just missed Sam in Australia but Milly was staying near Annie's. We arranged to meet at a hotel halfway. I was perplexed why Milly seemed on edge but, on reflection, we'd only met once and I was probably older than her mother. Before she won the competition, Milly had planned to work for a few months in Australia, and she'd tied this in with her trip.

'I hate writing the weekly reports,' she confessed. 'There is a limit to how many ways you can describe working and partying. All the interesting stuff has to be left out.'

'I wish I had that problem.' I muttered.

I admired Milly's courage in undertaking her journey alone at the age of nineteen – it was scary enough at fifty-one.

Two tasks remained before I flew to New Zealand: to thank Annie for her uncomplicated hospitality and to go to the Sydney Opera House, both achieved by buying tickets for a Nigel Kennedy concert. What better way to end my stay in Australia than with a dose of flamboyant musical virtuosity followed by champagne on the balcony of the Opera House overlooking the illuminated river and Sydney Harbour Bridge?

I was now more than halfway through my time as a Netjetter. Before Sydney, the days and weeks had stretched endlessly in front of me on my voyage of discovery. Was it only three months ago that I was at work? How could time have slipped by so quickly? What would I do when it ended? Confused and a little upset, I took stock. The few moments of fear, loneliness and panic hadn't sent me home, and they were far outweighed by the excitement of new places, people and experiences. My age was only occasionally a problem for me, but apparently it wasn't for anyone else, and I was getting better at mixing, particularly with the youngsters, which was invigorating, if often noisy. On balance I was doing fine. No, I thought, why worry now? There was still half the world to go.

9

Splendid Isolation

In Auckland, New Zealand, I stepped out of the airport into the rain – not refreshing tropical rain but chilly, miserable rain – and quickly rummaged in my big bag for the long trousers and thick jumper that I hadn't worn since the mountains in Nepal.

The quest for a comfy bed led me to the Auckland home of Lucy and John, friends of a friend from Ely. Lucy had emigrated several years before, swapping the flat, black landscape of East Anglia for the green hills and rain of New Zealand, and had met John there. I was waved inside by the wand of five-year-old Bella who, with a mop of blonde curls, a bedraggled tutu and a firm belief she was a fairy, generously lent me her bed.

The memory of tour buses through Australia was still fresh, so I decided to hire a car for my three weeks in New Zealand, as the distances seemed manageable. I set off into town, telling Lucy and John I'd be back late afternoon and, after some tough negotiation at the car rentals, signed all the papers and got into my smart new saloon.

'There are only two pedals,' I proclaimed in horror.

'It's an automatic,' the garage-man replied wearily. 'They only have two.'

'I do know that but I don't want an automatic. Can I have an un-automatic, please?'

'That means doing all the paperwork again,' muttered the garage man as he went to change the car.

By the time I left, darkness had joined the heavy rain outside. It was only as I screeched off the forecourt that it occurred to me that I had no idea how to get to the house. A termite-like instinct led me to the right district but locating the house proved a lot more difficult. It was definitely a right turn off the main street but after taking each right turn at least twice, I was dizzy from going in circles and still lost. When I eventually turned right much further down the road and found the house, a worried Lucy let me in two-and-a-half hours after I'd picked up the car – a mere fifteen minutes' drive away. There was great relief all round, with only a quiet mutter from John that he had a stack of maps, if only I'd asked.

New Zealand was wet. There had been rain in Asia: short, sharp showers that disappeared as quickly as they arrived, surface water vanishing in a trice and leaving behind a fresh cleanliness, however temporary. Auckland's rain was persistent and relentless, blanketing the city and obscuring the surrounding volcanic hills. I delayed my departure south for a day and dripped around the pleasant, if unremarkable, city seeking shelter in bookshops, coffee shops and internet cafés. As South America was only a few weeks away, the time to get to grips with some basic Spanish was long overdue and I bought a tape, Get by in Latin-American Spanish.

∞

The next morning, fearful of wasting my three weeks in New Zealand waiting for dry weather, I decided to press on regardless and head south. My plan was to cross to the South Island before the coming Easter rush and spend a week there before returning to the islands north of Auckland.

Two hours on the road and the rain finally stopped; at last, I could see the famous scenery of New Zealand. The rounded hills and fertile plains of this inland area reminded me of home and the South Downs where I grew up but, as I approached the geothermal area of Rotorua, all comparisons ceased.

Rotorua, nicknamed 'sulphur city', is in the middle of a lively volcanic area where lakes fill the holes left by geothermal activity. Wisps of steam from the hot spots below the city wafted up from streets and gardens, as if a hundred kettles on the boil had been buried, filling the air with a distinctive sulphurous smell that caught in the nose. Choosing a particularly steamy hostel, aptly named Hot Rocks, I visited the natural steam baths but sitting alone in large steel vat wasn't appealing, so I gave it a miss.

∞

The next morning, I was at the Wai-O-Tapu Thermal Wonderland just in time for the 10.15am daily eruption of the Lady Knox Geyser. It wasn't nature that was so punctual, but rather a mere mortal who poured biodegradable soap into the crater to break down the surface tension, thus producing a fifty-foot plume of boiling liquid. It reminded me of the time I accidentally removed the valve of a pressure cooker full of beetroot, releasing a hissing fountain of steam that showered me and my kitchen in a purple haze.

The trail around the park led to collapsed craters and sunken pools of thick oozing, glugging mud that bubbled and spat angrily. Large lakes of lurid green water edged with orange gave off steamy clouds of smelly vapour that hovered menacingly overhead. The vivid colours of the landscape, picked up from the elements and minerals of the rocks below – red from iron oxide, purple from manganese, lime green from arsenic, orange from antimony and black from sulphur – put any Jackson Pollock painting to shame.

This place, with a biblical glimpse of the fire and brimstone of hell, the overpowering smell, the turbulence and the exaggerated, unnatural colour, was unlike anything I'd experienced before. Until now I'd taken the solidity of the earth for granted, oblivious to the subterranean maelstrom. It was a sobering experience and I walked gingerly along the path, afraid the earth's crust might give way beneath my feet at any moment.

This area of New Zealand is of great significance to the Maori people and to ground myself, I booked a seat on a coach from the hostel to a Maori village nearby for a concert of singing and dance followed by a hangi, a traditional Maori feast. Initially dismayed by the dozen coaches rolling up and the Disneyworld feel of the village, I decided I might as well join in the fun of the traditional Maori greeting that involved lots of sticking-out of tongues and shouting.

The show of music and dance by handsome Maori men and women in grass skirts included a fearsome haka. These beefy men, like a dozen night-club bouncers throwing a tantrum, made English Morris men with their bells and sticks seem like ballet dancers. The delicious feast of lamb cooked in the earth in large clay ovens was accompanied by so much wine that the communal singing on the coach back was almost bearable.

∞

Having arranged to meet Mike and Claire, my travelling companions in India, in Wellington the next afternoon, I zipped through the next twenty-four hours at rally speed. I lapped Lake Taupo before roaring along the winding hilly roads across the Tongariro National Park. Fortunately the roads were empty as I negotiated the bends and glimpsed views of the tall, snow-crusted peaks of three volcanoes that towered in the distance.

Ohakune had seemed a good place to stop but with no hostels or even shops open, I drove on towards the West Coast. Whanganui was like a frontier town in a Western just before the baddies rode in; the streets were deserted, the shops shut and only the tumbleweed was missing. Hungry and fed up with my own company, I booked into a hostel and went in search of food. Unable to find any cafés or restaurants, I knew the Chinese wouldn't let me down and, sure enough, I soon found a takeaway, where a cook took my order in a strange flat-vowelled 'Chin-kiwi' accent: 'Meal for whon – that will be sex dollars.'

There was enough rice and chow mein for a brace of Maori warriors, so I offered a share to the backpackers in the hostel kitchen. They were a monosyllabic lot, infected by the same introversion as the town. They all refused politely and carried on stirring their packet noodles, taking them off to their rooms, leaving me alone in the kitchen pining for the jolly, gregarious hostels of Borneo. As the weeks went on, this was to be the pattern of my New Zealand experience.

∞

The drive down the west coast to Wellington the next morning was uneventful, until the car suddenly emitted a loud grinding noise that stopped as suddenly as it had started. After pulling up and looking at the engine – a token gesture, as the wires, boxes and tubes under a bonnet might just as well be a nuclear reactor as far as I was concerned – I shrugged and drove on, ignoring the slightly strange steering.

The scenery had changed from the wild, craggy hills of the National Park to gentler, rounded hills that looked worn and parched. At the same time, the trees had red and gold leaves. It had taken me nearly a week to grasp that this was April and therefore autumn. Although delighted to have avoided winter at home, I felt a sudden pang of homesickness as I thought of the daffodils, tulips and fruit blossom of British springtime.

In Wellington that afternoon, Mike and Claire took me to a hill that overlooked the city and the Marlborough Sounds.

'What a view, but why is everything so brown?' I asked.

'New Zealand has been suffering a severe drought.'

'No one told Auckland.'

We reminisced about India and the events of the last two months over a meal of lamb and wine. Mike's skills as a food technician had been transported from Wotsits in Wales to Whittaker's in Wellington. Whittaker's was the chunkiest, nicest chocolate I'd tasted in three months. No wonder Mike never lost any weight.

∞

Mike and Claire brought me a cup of tea early in the morning, said goodbye and went off to work, but the unfamiliar after-effects of wine meant I slept until midday. Hastily throwing all my things into my bag and shutting the front door firmly behind me, I unlocked the car and turned the key in the ignition. Silence. The engine was as dead as Whanganui, leaving me stranded with no phone, no way back into Mike and Claire's house and a ferry to catch to the South Island.

The residential neighbourhood was deserted, only one open front door hinting at life. When I knocked on it the lady of the house, with all the charm of a deep freezer, brought out her phone for me to call for help. As I sat in the car to wait and absently turned the key, the roar of the engine so surprised me that I hit my head on the roof. Not daring to bother the sullen woman again, I drove off in search of a phone box to cancel the call-out.

This incident persuaded me that I must get the car fixed and I drove to the Wellington office of the hire firm. The mechanic came out from under the bonnet shaking his head. 'Well m'dear, the power-steering cable is completely mangled up in the engine.'

'Is that unusual?'

'In all my years as a mechanic, I've never seen it before.'

'Wow!' I said. 'Another first. Can you fix it in time for me to get the ferry in an hour?'

'No way! We'll give you another car.'

As he went to fetch another set of keys, I shouted, 'Three pedals, please!'

∞

As darkness obscured the Marlborough Sounds during the crossing, it wasn't until I set off in the morning along the scenic coast road from the hostel in Picton that I could enjoy the views of the craggy islands covered in forest and rock that rose out of the dark blue water. I was on my way to Richmond, near Nelson, to stay with Margaret, my ex-boyfriend Philip's ex-wife's cousin – possibly the most convoluted of all the connections used to gain a bed.

I'd started the day as a happy, healthy human but by the time the sun set I'd morphed into a spluttering bag of germs, a stream of snot dribbling from my nose, eyes like currants inside puffballs, ears buzzing with the sound of a thousand insects and teeth aching in sympathy. What Margaret thought of this wretched wreck arriving on her doorstep she kept to herself, but from my point of view it was the right time to be ill, in a proper house with an attentive host dispensing Lemsip and TLC.

Margaret was a down-to-earth New Zealander in her sixties married to Ross, a Maori, who was away visiting his ancestral land on one of the islands in the Sounds. Their son, Michael, a good-looking chap of thirty with a passion for field sports, was home from the island and we showed each other our photos.

'That's me with a deer I shot,' said Michael proudly.

'Mmm, dat's a big one,' I croaked, trying to stop my nose dripping onto the print.

'Nah, that's a baby, just look at this son of a bitch.'

As my fragile stomach turned at all this dead flesh, Margaret came to my rescue by changing the subject. 'Do you know any young single women? The only criterion is the ability to skin and fillet.'

'Fraid nut,' I answered from behind a wad of tissues.

∞

As I was feeling slightly better in the morning, Margaret and her sister Cynthia took me on a 'tiki tour' – just going where the fancy takes you. It took us first to a Japanese park in Nelson and then to the ancestral meeting place of Ross's Maori tribe, where the carved gateposts, guarded by fearsome monsters with their tongues hanging out to frighten off enemies and evil spirits, told the story of the people. I wrote Bruce into tribal folk law by taking his picture amongst the carvings.

At a cliff-top beauty spot, overlooking picture-postcard bays of blue sea and golden sand, the sisters produced a bountiful picnic which they laid out on a checked tablecloth

– a little bit of England transported to the other side of the world. As I waved them goodbye, once again I marvelled at the kindness of total strangers.

∞

To see as much as possible of the South Island, I'd marked off the beauty spots and national parks, allocating them part of a day and a night each. The schedule was tight, with a lot of driving, but I figured I could do it in a week.

First stop was the Abel Tasman National Park, a stretch of coast with a four-day walk through bush and along cliffs overlooking quiet sandy bays. An alternative was to kayak the length of the park but, for those lacking time or fitness like me, water taxis hopped between the bays. In the morning, my water taxi set off at high speed and crashed through the waves, causing a few kayakers along the way to wobble precariously. Dropped off at Bark Bay, it was good to use the legs again on a beautiful walk in bright, warm sun. The path took me through rich woodland, up rocky outcrops with panoramic views and down into sandy bays where I could rest and read.

It was out of season and very quiet, and the only person I met was a young lad with a huge rucksack. I wondered why he was stumbling and looking so pained until I saw that he was walking in his socks.

'Are you OK?' I asked.

'Bad feet. How far is it to the hostel?'

I had been walking for over an hour but, to give him heart, I told him that it was only thirty minutes away. Once again I blessed my walking boots, super-comfy even if no longer waterproof. Six miles further along the coast the boat was waiting for me at Anchorage Bay

I'd begun to doubt the wisdom of my gruelling schedule but set off again in the late afternoon for the Nelson Lakes National Park. Darkness fell swiftly, making map-reading difficult and panicking me into turning off the main road too early and onto a poor road that degenerated into an unmade track. With no light from habitation, the cloudy sky or even another car, my headlights bored into an inky blackness that you rarely see in the heavily populated British Isles. Realising how much we take white lines and cat's eyes for granted, I convinced myself that I was on the road to nowhere, so sighed with relief when the welcoming lights of the village of St. Arnaud finally appeared.

∞

After a quick look round this area of deep-blue lakes ringed by beech forest and the humped brown mountains characteristic of the South Island, I headed west to the coast. On the narrow road that wound through the dark, forbidding rock of Buller Gorge, only tall grass lay between the road that hugged the mountainside and the deep gorge with a river at the bottom. At Hawk's Gap, a passage that had been literally hacked out of rock, a low ledge hanging over the road formed a tunnel on three sides. I stopped briefly to look at a bungee-jumping site, a terrifying leap off a bridge into the gorge.

Wondering what would possess anyone in his or her right mind to undertake such an activity, I was struck by my own insanity. Why was I in such a rush? What was the point of skimming over this land at such a pace? I'd not stopped to appreciate the Marlborough Sounds, had sped through two outstandingly beautiful areas, both of which merited weeks of exploration, and was now dashing through spectacular mountains.

Throughout most of my trip, the time spent in each country was too short; three weeks in New Zealand was as optimistic as trying to see London in an hour. Compromise was called for and I determined from that moment to slow down, abandoning any idea of going to the islands north of Auckland so I could spend more time enjoying the South Island. When I set off again, it felt like a huge weight had been lifted as I now felt free to stop and admire the views along the west coast road as it followed the sea, twisting along precipitous cliffs overlooking huge waves crashing among the jagged rocks below.

Instead of pressing on to Greymouth, I took my first tiki tour to look at Punakaiki, and in particular an area known as the Pancake Rocks. The dark grey limestone rocks were built up in thin layers like stacks of tortillas, holes worn in them by the action of the sea; at high tide the sea thunders in and shoots up through the gaps. Mesmerised, I watched as each incoming wave produced a cascade of plumes, like the climax to a fireworks' display, with a multitude of mini-rainbows as the sunlight caught the droplets. I stayed until the tide retreated beyond the rocks.

Greymouth lived up to its name; it's only redeeming was feature a fish-and-chip shop where I wolfed down my first chips since leaving home.

∞

The glacial region was next on the itinerary. Here, the Franz Josef and Fox, the two biggest glaciers in New Zealand, flow into rainforest to create an ecosystem unique to this land.

Having enjoyed lovely sunshine since leaving Auckland, the weather turned and I arrived at the town of Franz Josef in pouring rain, with thick grey mist obscuring the glacier. The hostel was littered with wet clothing and grumpy hikers, and the air was thick with the Darwinesque smell of damp socks. In the stuffy four-bed room, with the heater on full to dry clothes, my cold re-emerged, and I slept fitfully until I was woken in the night by an exasperated, angry scream.

'For Christ's sake, stop that fucking snoring!'

My blocked nose and the total absence of saliva in my desert-like mouth meant I couldn't avoid the painful truth – it was me. My world was shattered and, mortified, I retreated deep into my sleeping bag until dawn.

In the morning I rushed out to send an important email to my friend Philip, whom I could trust to give an honest answer to the important question: Do I snore?

∞

A cloudless blue sky meant that the 'heli-hike' I'd booked the day before could go ahead, the perfect distraction while the answer to my question flew through the ether. Kitted out in spiked boots, pickaxe and gloves, a helicopter was ready to take the group onto the glacier.

This was my first flight in a helicopter and I was filled with a childlike excitement as I climbed into the small and frail bubble under the powerful rotors. An apocalyptic staccato whirl of blades took us swiftly up and we banked at steep angles between the ice-covered mountainsides. If ever I win the lottery or a long-lost aunt leaves me a fortune, I will buy a helicopter – I loved it.

Dropped off on a high ridge, the prospect of walking across the ice was very frightening, but if I could scuba dive I could tackle anything. After practising securing footholds on the hard, wet ice using the axe as balance and to test the ground, we gingerly hiked up a hill. Once I forgot that this was slippery ice and remembered to stamp the spikes down hard, walking was relatively easy, although the occasional deep crevice that crossed our path was scary.

Amid the glaring whiteness, cracks and holes were filled with an eerie blue hue. We hiked to a series of ice caves that glowed with blue light, turning to a bright aquamarine in the deeper recesses. The caves, which appear in the ice each day, were located early in the morning by the guides, who marked them and hacked out steps, ready to overwhelm the likes of me with fairy-tale hollows and tunnels.

We were all on a high as we slid and crawled through these sapphire warrens. Two hours flew by before our helicopter arrived to take us back to earth. This walk on the ice truly connected me with New Zealand. I wasn't just admiring the scenery while speeding through it on four wheels.

After a steak sandwich the size of a Sunday joint, I rushed to the nearest internet café to check for that crucial email from Philip. There it was, and I opened it with trembling fingers.

'Sue, you have been known to snore occasionally but I always found it yet another of your endearing qualities. Love

Philip'

Only Philip could break this news in a positive way and, sitting in an internet café thousands of miles from home, I missed him. As always, I was bemused by our parting as he was one of a rare breed: a genuinely nice bloke. Something in my make up makes me dissatisfied with 'nice,' especially if it is linked to a passion for folk music.

It took a while to recover from the shocking news that I was a snorer, so it was already late afternoon before I set off for Wanaka, driving along mountain passes in the direction of the setting sun. Kiwi mountain roads are one-way over bridges or through particularly narrow passes, which is fine if you can see ahead of you but, blinded by the low sun, I just put my trust in luck.

Arriving in Wanaka later than expected, I stopped at my chosen hostel and was surprised to see a sign on the door saying 'Full'; on to the next – 'Full'; and the next – 'Full, Full and Full.' Had the population of Auckland decamped south, en masse, to escape the rain? However, I realised it was Good Friday; Easter weekend was obviously busy in Wanaka.

It was looking as if I would have to spend my first night in the car when I spotted a little B&B down a side road. Without much hope of success, I knocked on the door. Although it too was full, the kind landlady telephoned an emergency B&B number and found a bed at a farm a couple of miles outside the town – but at double the B&B norm and quintuple what a hostel would have cost. Not having eaten, I checked the cash situation to find that the cost of the bed would clean me out and at 10.30pm there wasn't much chance of cashing travellers' cheques. I would just have to go hungry.

The B&B was luxurious, with an immaculate cream carpet, sparking white bed linen, a dozen plump pillows and a thick virgin-white towel, all waiting desecration by my dusty boots and body. Already intimidated by this cleanliness, I was taunted by the smell of newly baked hot cross buns wafting from the kitchen. A jug of coffee was brought to my room but no bun accompanied it, and I fell into bed salivating.

At breakfast, my hosts were amazed by the quantity of hot cross buns, croissants and toast I packed away. When it was time to pay, I don't know if it was because of this obvious starvation, but the price was dropped to the B&B norm. The reason for Wanaka's shortage of beds was that the rodeo was in town and, happy to chalk up yet another first, I hitched up my trousers and headed for the fun.

The crowd sported so many Stetsons, checked shirts and gingham dresses, with the odd spur jangling off fancy cowboy boots, that I expected a banjo to start up and the audience to 'yee-ha' and form lines. Instead, I discovered that the roping of steers, bucking of broncos and racing of cowgirls was a deadly serious and competitive business. It was also riveting and I became absorbed in watching man against beast, thighs desperately clamped against angry horseflesh, rope spinning to lasso the horns of massive bulls, and pretty girls urging on horses as if possessed by demons.

I tore myself away in the late afternoon to reach the adrenaline capital of the world, Queenstown, where I'd taken the precaution of pre-booking a room – a single room.

∞

I wandered around this tourist centre on Easter Sunday, trying to decide which of the potentially lethal and very expensive activities to try. Bungee jumping was out, skydiving was too expensive, I didn't fancy quad bikes down vertical mountains, so that left a jet boat ride down the river. Kitted out in a yellow lifejacket, I felt rather self-conscious as the only person over twenty-five in the group photo. The boat roared off across the lake and down the river. The water was very low because of the drought and rushing at the river bank before turning through 360 degrees in a foot of water was rather lame. No chocolate eggs for me this Sunday – only a parking ticket on my car.

With only a week left in New Zealand, I reluctantly turned north again to begin the long drive back. That evening I booked into Killermont Station, on the road to Christchurch, described in the guidebook as 'peaceful'. The cosy farmhouse looked very inviting but, instead of ushering me in, the landlady instructed me to follow her car. Miles along a rough track, we stopped outside a far-from-cosy corrugated shed with windows – once, I guess, a shearer's hut.

'You can pay me now and just leave in the morning when you feel like it.'

'Is there anyone else staying?'

'No, just you, dear.'

'Where's the key?'

'Key? You're perfectly safe out here, dear,' she shouted as she drove off.

I felt very vulnerable in the middle of an empty expanse that even the sheep had deserted, with no lock on the door and no phone, but as it was now pitch-black outside and I was far from a town of any size, there was little choice but to stay.

The interior of the shed was homely, with carpets and an electric fire in the living room, two double bedrooms, a shower and a washing machine with an ancient mangle that could have graced any antique shop. Luckily I had an emergency packet of noodles, some Whittaker's and a jar of instant coffee in my bag, so at least there was the option of pasta with chocolate or coffee sauce. I found a cassette player in the lounge and I put on Get by in Latin-American Spanish, hoping the conversation would make the place less lonesome.

'Hola, me llamo José.'

'Hola, me llamo Sue'

'Que quieres tomar?'

'Quiero a bloody large whiskey, por favor!'

I couldn't concentrate on this, so tried reading the visitors' book instead, immediately identifying with another lone traveller who had written: 'This is a lovely place but I could sure do with some company.'

Preparations for the night included moving the heavy kitchen table against the door, finding the biggest kitchen knife to have beside me and choosing the bedroom that had a bolt. I consoled myself that I could snore as loudly as I liked as there didn't even appear to be any sheep to disturb.

My life so far had been mundane and without fear. There had been odd moments, like the trips to casualty to have my accident-prone son Sam's head sewn up, or arriving home alone from the shops having set out hours before with three-year-old Rachel in her pushchair. (I'd left her in a supermarket, where I subsequently found her sobbing pitifully surrounded by tutting ladies.)

Here, alone in the middle of empty countryside, the anxiety was acute and prolonged and produced a dull ache in my chest and the pit of my stomach, making it difficult to breathe or swallow. Despite all the precautions, once I was in bed my senses were on red alert, registering every creak and squeak for miles around. Sleep came in short, fitful bursts and when I was awake I repeatedly reassured myself by touching the knife under the pillow.

Morning was a relief and daylight changed isolation into beauty as I ate breakfast outside in the sun, surrounded by sweeping hills in the now-unthreatening peace and quiet.

∞

Knowing that my nerves couldn't hold out for another night, I set off again for Christchurch, where the punts on the river reminded me of Cambridge. Choosing an all-female hostel with single rooms for the first time since arriving in New Zealand, I spent the evening chatting with fellow travellers.

I don't know if it was because I was travelling by car or because everyone spoke English so there was no need to seek out company, but I'd found New Zealand hostels lonely and quiet, without the friendliness of Asian ones. This was the first country as a Netjetter where I'd had no travelling companions. It was bearable most of the time but eating alone night after night was not, and I often felt the urge to accost strangers and force them at knifepoint to join my table. Fortunately I had, however, lost my brand new Swiss army knife to the airport staff at Kathmandu airport.

In contrast, this hostel was welcoming and relaxing, run by a German woman who took pains to introduce us to each other. The only drawback was its pinkness – wallpaper, bedding, towels in a variety of sickly shades. Despite that, I stayed on an extra day to talk, have a rest and replenish the stores.

∞

I resumed my headlong rush across the land with an overnight stop in Kaikoura, where unfortunately a whale-watching trip I'd booked was cancelled. Kaikoura, a small coastal town with dolphins and whales off its coast but little else, didn't take long to explore, so I wandered back to the hostel where the balcony was dominated by a crowd of English youngsters discussing their A-level results.

Feeling tired after being on the move for the last four months, I felt the onset of another of the 'old moments' that I'd experienced periodically, especially in Australia, when I was constantly surrounded by youth and energy. I felt irrationally angry with these youngsters who were so absorbed in discussing their bright futures that they hadn't time for the old biddy at the edge of the group. Knowing that I'd have been the same at their age didn't soothe my growing desire for attention so, rather than scream at them, I went for a walk.

Kaikora was too remote for the internet, my usual antidote to such moods, so I went to bed in low spirits, not improved by the 'noise' from the couple next door. That evening I badly missed the comfort and warmth of a hug, a kiss, any human touch, but I may have got my own back on my neighbours with my world-renowned snoring.

Overnight stops with Mike and Claire and John and Lucy were oases of normality and company on the long journey back to Auckland to catch the next flight. When I returned the car, the garage man raised his eyebrows at the different model and the money for the parking fine that I'd left in the glove compartment, but made no comment.

Despite the whirlwind progress and lack of company, New Zealand was a fantastic country – breathtakingly beautiful and with a different vista round each bend. Now I was about to embark on the final stage of my journey: South America, another new and unknown continent. There wasn't a single relative, friend of friends or website contact waiting anywhere to take me in and, despite good intentions, I hadn't got past the first chapter in learning Spanish.

I was terrified.

10

'¿Hola, Habla Inglés?'

It had been a long day, or more correctly two calendar days, with the bizarre experience of setting off from New Zealand on Sunday afternoon and arriving in Argentina on Sunday morning. From the moment I booked the trip, I'd been nervous about South America – it was so far away and not on the well-travelled backpacker route – and, landing in Buenos Aires, I felt the same stomach-churning sickness as I had arriving in Mumbai.

Yet I'd become a very different traveller from the one who'd set off nearly five months before: physically leaner, fitter, swarthier, if somewhat scruffier and badly in need of a haircut and, last but by no means least, sporting excellent squatting muscles. My confidence had outgrown even my hair, as now I was unfazed by touts, hadn't been blessed for ages, and no longer batted an eyelid at sharing a room with strapping lads in their underpants. Thus a new assurance was fighting a rear-guard action against gnawing anxiety as I gave the taxi driver the address of my hotel and we sped through that big city.

South America seemed to favour cheap hotels rather than hostels for travellers, but beware all web descriptions! In Auckland I'd found a Buenos Aires hotel on the internet and, in my very first attempt to speak Spanish, telephoned to book what I had hoped was a room rather than a kilo of oranges.

The Metropolitan Hotel, much further from the centre than expected, may have been 'grande' several generations before but had degenerated into a decaying edifice that reeked of bottled gas. For 'kitchen' read one blackened gas ring, for 'laundry room' read one large chipped sink, for 'lounge area' read ancient stained settee and for 'English-speaking' read lie.

After dragging my big bag up several flights of narrow stairs, I was shown into a grubby little room containing an ancient bed and plywood wardrobe, with a bathroom down the hall. The only other guest was an unshaven young Argentine, who spoke no English. As I lay on the bed, jetlagged and unsure if the prickliness of my skin was due to tiredness or bed bugs, my heart sank and I felt very far from home. After an hour of staring at the faded wallpaper, I grabbed Bruce and my day bag.

'Come on, little bear,' I announced. 'We've only got four weeks in this continent and that's an hour of it gone. Let's go explore.'

Right next to the hotel was the Subte, or Underground, and I approached the man in the booth.

'Boleto, por favor,' I asked confidently, having looked up the word for ticket before setting out, only to be answered by a torrent of incomprehensible Spanish accompanied by much gesticulation. My blank look only encouraged the man to raise the volume and increase the arm-waving, until in desperation I shoved the guidebook's underground map under his nose and pointed at my randomly chosen station. With a sigh of exasperation he thrust a handful of tokens at me and snatched my crisp new note. Waiting for the train, I saw that no one actually bought tickets, only tokens from a machine – well, how was I to know?

Alighting at Calle Florida, I entered a smart pedestrianised area. This was central Buenos Aires, with its rows of boutiques, coffee shops and restaurants. With patterned paving, troughs of potted plants and modern lampposts, it could have been a precinct in Madrid, Rome, any modern city, but the people were absent – this shopping and eating heart of Buenos Aires was closed. Argentina, a good Catholic nation, observed the Sabbath, making my extra-long Sunday very quiet.

I ate in a pizza restaurant, not quite Argentine haute

cuisine, but it was the only place open and my feeble Spanish didn't matter there. Anxious to find better accommodation, half a block away a small door on the street led me into the Maipu Hotel, another large, rambling place with a cavernous hallway, its faded elegance reflecting a decline into the backpacker market. No English was spoken here either, but my mañana seemed to be understood. Too tired to take in this new city and new continent, I made my way back to the Metropolitan, where I barricaded myself in my room and sank onto the lumpy bed.

∞

The next morning, the breakfast included in the price of the room turned out to be a voucher to cash in at an international burger chain across the road. In five months I'd made it a point of principle never to eat at these places, or the even more prolific fried chicken takeaways that had spread like a pandemic across the world. On my first full day on this continent, I faced a moral dilemma and a hollow belly; pragmatism defeated principle as I scoffed my three baby croissants and gulped down the disgusting coffee.

Taking a taxi to escape the scene of my fast-food crime, I dumped my bags at the Maipu and headed out into weekday Buenos Aires. Sunday had passed and I'd had eleven hours sleep, so both the city and I had come alive. The narrow streets were choked with yellow taxis, adding thick diesel fumes to the whiff of bottled gas that seemed to permeate the air in the streets as well as in the hotels, and people thronged the narrow pavements in a noisy, fast-moving stream. Everybody seemed to know everybody else, and the path would typically be blocked as people stopped to plant kisses on each other's cheeks and exchange animated greetings in a torrent of loud, rapid Spanish. I'd already realised that my one lesson on the tape was going to be as much use as my long-forgotten Latin A level.

Buenos Aires seemed a different type of city from any I had been in so far, as vibrant and noisy as those in Asia but

Kakadu swimming hole

Above: Kevin and Ricky

Below: Kakadu rock art

Above: Devil's Marbles

Below: Ayres Rock

Above: Scuba Dive on the Great Barrier Reef

Below: Bruce in front of Sydney Opera House

Above: Daintree

Below: Bondi Beach

Above: Wai-O-Taou

Below: Abel Tasman National Park

Punakaiki

Above: Franz Josef Glacier

Below: Ice Walking (Franz Josef Glacier)

without the cows and beggars, and much older than those in Australasia. The smattering of old Spanish-influenced buildings between the modern office blocks and trendy restaurants gave it the dilapidated but proud air of an old European capital. The quiet, empty roads and undemonstrative people of New Zealand were a long way away.

I walked back to the shopping area to get my bearings, where the designer boutiques, cafés, cake shops and ice-cream parlours were now open and packed with Argentines. With my straggly hair and faded clothes, I felt very scruffy amongst these tall, handsome, well-dressed people. From the perspective of my own generation, I was struck by the older men, who obviously took pains to preserve themselves there wasn't a potbelly in sight under the flashy suits.

The one thing Buenos Aires had in common with Asia was the proliferation of shoeshine boys but here, rather than chasing you to polish your flip-flops, they all seemed to have customers – businessmen sitting in the chairs reading their newspapers while their Italian leather shoes were made to gleam.

Argentina would easily win any prize for the best coffee shops, which were oases of calm with no pressure to leave once you'd drunk your coffee and eaten the accompanying free cake or biscuit. Although they were perfect places to sit and people-watch, my hope that another lone traveller might wander in and keep me company was never realised. The conversations around me were always in quick-fire Spanish that I had no hope of following.

It was an absurd thought that years before we'd been at war with these people over the Falklands, but there was no obvious sign of any lingering resentment. The one exception was on a board in a bureau de change where the little Union Jack next to sterling had been scratched out.

I walked down the long Avenida de San Martin to the Plaza de Mayo, the heart of the city. Impressive state buildings including the cathedral, the Cabildo, the town hall and the Casa de Gobierno or Casa Rosada, a pink palace that contains the presidential offices, surrounded the square decorated with giant palms and statues on plinths. Every Thursday the mothers of 'The Disappeared', young men who vanished during the repressive regime of the 1970s, walk round the plaza with pictures of their sons pinned to their chests. Although on this Monday the mothers were absent, there were still political speakers, stalls and policemen, and the pictures of the missing adorned the railings around the monument in the centre of the square. Even without the mothers, the plaza reeked of pain; each photo showed a young person whose promise would never be realised.

That evening I tried my first Argentine steak and, although it was only a small, unpretentious restaurant, my table had an elegant chintz cloth and a waiter in black suit and waistcoat hovered nearby. Maybe I should have been wary as I seemed to be the only customer ordering food, with all the others sitting over drinks.

The first mouthful of my steak might have been the remains of a stray dog marinated in axle grease. The waiter's smile didn't falter as he brought me the bottle of wine included in the meal while I checked in my little dictionary that bife de lomo didn't mean 'only to only be fed to animals and non-Spanish-speaking tourists'. Afraid of the likely future effects of the meat, I ate the vegetables and downed all the wine. Without sufficient food to counter the alcohol, when I got up to leave the room was swaying as if I was doing a solo tango. How shad, I thought – the only time on the trip that I'm totally pished and I've only got a teddy bear for company. After a few strange looks from passers-by as I wove my way along the street, I took refuge in an internet café and wrote garbled emails to a few carefully chosen friends.

∞

The next day I set out to walk beyond the centre, aiming to reach the barrios or the district of La Boca, the artistic heart of the city. Avoiding the most direct route, the Avenida 9 de Julio, a sixteen-lane highway, I wandered down the Av Bolivar, getting both a history and geography lesson as I crossed the Avs Belgrano, Venezuela, México, Chile and Independencia. I walked along wide avenues past tall skyscrapers, faded hotels and town houses until I reached the cobbled streets and colourful old Rosista houses of San Telmo.

I sat among the crowd relaxing in the Plaza Dorrego, lined with antique shops, little cafés and art shops. In a pavement café served by the now-familiar besuited waiter, I tried to order iced fruit juice but had got my hielo and my helado mixed up and ended up with a warm drink and an ice-cream. Such is life.

As I was crunching the end of my cone, a couple began to dance the tango in the square. I was excited because a tango evening had been on my list of things to do but I hadn't met anyone and was too nervous to go on my own. The couple were both well into the third age, the man full of a bravado that defied his faded appearance and the woman disguising the ravages of time with a trowel-full of make-up. Despite the fact that their glory days might be over, they put on a fine show, dazzling me with the flamboyant dress, extravagant gestures and flashing feet of this wonderful dance. Even when danced by two geriatrics the tango was so sexy, so proud, so passionate, so ... Argentinian.

As soon as the couple finished, I felt isolated. The tango was not something to watch when you hadn't talked to anyone for days and the last kiss you had was from your daughter five months ago. I wanted to dance with a dashing Argentine, to feel that intimacy, to stick my chin out, stamp my feet and twirl – though it would have to be in bare feet, as walking boots would kill all passion. Sadly I knew it wouldn't happen and, as it was too late to carry on to La Boca, I walked back to the city centre beside the wide muddy estuary along the Puerto Madero.

The old dockyards had gone the way of many wharves around the world and were now fashionable upmarket restaurants and bars. Walking past the large glass windows where sophisticated Argentines were wining and dining, my feeling of disconnection and loneliness grew even stronger. This was too vibrant a city to visit on your own.

∞

With just over four weeks left in South America, and the lesson of the previous months at last sinking in that it was pointless to try to cover the whole continent, I was determined to limit myself to specific places. For the remaining time in Argentina I booked a three-night, two-day trip to the Iguazú Falls, on the border with Brazil, one of my more expensive jaunts at nearly $400. No discount available here, probably due to a shortage of local Guardian readers.

The local airport was far removed from its international big brother, a confusing, disorderly place that seemed to have been designed as a deliberate initiative test for non-Spanish-speaking tourists. I imagine various coach-loads of vacationers from Idaho and Hamburg are still scattered around the terminal, wandering endless corridors or trapped in a broom cupboard somewhere. It was only by thrusting my ticket at a harassed official that I was directed to the right queue. On the two-hour flight I waited anxiously to see where we would land, as it was just as likely to be Tierra del Fuego or the Malvinas as Iguazú.

Reassured when we did land at Iguazú, the next challenge was to find the coach. Luckily, the name of the travel company was emblazoned on the side and a loud, jolly rep was waiting.

'¿Hola, habla Inglés?' I asked my carefully rehearsed question.

'Ah Inglésa! No, disculpe,' came the disappointing reply.

While driving to the hotel, the rep began his speech.

'Hola, bienvenida. Iguazú es…' That was it, four words and he'd lost me. The rest listened intently, laughed in unison, scribbled down what appeared to be times, and once he'd finished began a buzz of conversation amongst themselves. I sat in ignorance, once more regretting my laziness in not learning more Spanish. Like one of the Pied Piper's rats, I followed the rep off the bus at the Brazilian border and straight into a foot bath, presumably to prevent the spread of exotic diseases.

While I was checking in at the hotel in Brazil (several stars more than my customary accommodation), one of the staff collected names, but I had no idea whether it was for dinner or to join the Brazilian army. 'Shall we go?' I heard in precise Surrey English behind me. Excited, I turned to see a middle-aged couple from the pages of Country Life, and explained my predicament. Their accompanying Argentine translator told me there was to be a dance show, the 'Spectacular', that evening in the village. As I had, more by accident than design, seen a dance show in every land, I signed up.

Mrs Surrey informed me they were on a South American tour demonstrating cake decorating, and images of Andean Indians sculpting Machu Picchu out of pink icing flashed through my mind. Her straight face and Women's Institute demeanour stifled my incipient giggle and I politely asked if cake decorating was big in South America.

'Yes, we are fully booked.'

Iguazú is on the border of Brazil, Argentina and Paraguay, and all the traditions of dance were represented at this glitzy affair. With no invitation to join the English couple, I sat alone watching Paraguayan folk dancing, Argentinian tango and Brazilian Mardi Gras, which featured long legs and big feathers. After the show, two of the female dancers in vertiginously high heels were in the foyer posing for photos. Feeling very silly, I waited until the crowd had thinned and gesticulated for one of them to pose kissing Bruce for the website. Kissing a little teddy bear was the probably the safest proposition the dancer had had that evening.

∞

We were to spend this first morning on the Argentinian side of the falls. Unable to learn about the area from the guide, I had to rely on the brief description in the guidebook.

'The River Iguazú, having gathered many tributaries in its 800-mile journey, plunges off the Parana Plateau along a crescent-shaped cliff two-and-a-half miles long. 275 waterfalls plunge into a rainforest area at the rate of 1,750 cubic metres a second.'

No words from guide or guidebook could have prepared me for the thunderous roar of falling water that could be heard several miles away, or for the multitude and magnitude of the falls.

We started at a lookout area with a panoramic view of dozens of falls crashing into the rivers and forest in a maelstrom of swirling water and spray. A walkway meandered along ridges, rising and falling so that the power and volume of the water at the top and the bottom of the falls could be seen close at hand. At some falls, the water plunged over the edge in solid sheets; at others it foamed angrily as it was diverted round protruding rocks, and in places it flowed down giant rock steps like a water slide. The white of the surging water contrasted with the grey of the rock and the dark green of the rainforest, with beautiful butterflies adding flashes of red, yellow and blue. During the preceding five months I'd seen mountains, deserts, rainforests, glaciers and geysers, but this display was of nature at its most powerful.

Stopping so many times to take photos and to greet a raccoon on the path, I lost the rest of my party but it didn't matter, as speech was lost in the sound of the falls. Eventually the guide found me and led me back to the rest of the group for lunch, where I had to find my translators again as there was more expedition organising. This time it was for 'The Great Adventure', a ride through the rainforest and then a jet boat up the river; ever game, I signed up.

The ride was in a 4x4 open lorry along muddy tracks, and the adventure started in earnest when the lorry broke down. The river wasn't far away and we could walk, so I was grateful for my trusty if leaky walking boots; those with less sturdy footwear were offered plastic bags to tie over their feet. A group of unruly macho Australian lads lost their swagger when struggling with supermarket bags round their sandals.

Divided into groups, we began the mile-long ride in jet

boats down the river to the base of the waterfalls. This was exciting stuff, careering along at high speed avoiding rapids, whirlpools and jagged rocks, and it was even better in the swirling water at the base of a huge fall. Breathless and soaking wet, we swept round a corner and under an even bigger waterfall. In the middle of this seething cauldron of wild, white foaming water and spray, under cascades of falling water, I yelled in exhilaration, but it was impossible to hear anything against the ear-shattering roar. When the driver reversed into calmer water and asked if we wanted to go round again, the passengers all responded without hesitation and off we sped back under the falls. In terms of adrenaline production this made the Queenstown boat ride seem like punting down the Cam. I was very wet and very happy.

∞

My English translators left the next morning, no doubt working on a meringue Iguazú Falls design. Seeing my look of bewilderment, a young pony-tailed Argentine, Pedro, adopted me and tried unsuccessfully to tell me what was going on. With just a phrase book between us, our attempts at conversation usually ended in good-humoured shrugging.

The walk around this Brazilian side of the falls was even more spectacular, the waterfalls bigger and more numerous. At one point there was a walkway right into the centre of an area into which falls from every direction merged into a swirling basin. I took one of my five-second videos with the digital camera and, although I could only capture a quarter of the scene due to the spray, I caught one of the many rainbows produced by the sun and spray.

After the walk, confident that I'd understood we were to meet up again at 1.30pm, I was having a coffee watching the carpet of butterflies when Pedro ran up. Appointed by the coach as my minder, he'd been sent to find me when the bus was ready to leave – at 11.30am. There was an ironic cheer from the other passengers as we got back on the bus and I adopted my best 'sorry, I'm a foreigner' smile.

At lunch we sat with another coach party, which included a woman who could speak English. Pedro and I had spent half an hour miming our occupations but we'd both been baffled, me by his wild hacking motions, and he by my attempt to mime dragging children back to school. With the help of our translator, I learnt that he was in charge of the meat department of a supermarket, but I don't think he was any the wiser as to what I did.

∞

Back in the capital, I wrote my report a day late for the very first time; until then I'd always managed to find a computer on a Friday. It didn't matter so much as there'd been changes back at the Guardian around Easter when Imogen, my editor, had left and a new name, Gwynn, appeared on the emails. Since then, my reports no longer appeared on the website for Saturday but might appear anytime up to Wednesday the following week, and they were much more heavily edited; previously my reports had been virtually untouched. The photos of the Franz Josef glacier had also been lost but I wasn't too upset as I always copied them back home to my friend and travel addict, Rosy. There seemed to have been a change not only in personnel but in interest. Alone for so long, this weakening of a link, even through cyberspace, upset me, as I had met Imogen and knew she was flesh and blood.

It was only when I retrieved my big bag from the storeroom at the Maipu that I realised I was missing my sleeping bag. The man at the desk took a while to understand my constant repetition of, 'Dónde saco? Saco? Saco de dormir?' even slipping into 'saco losto' in my agitation. He shook his head and, although we checked the store cupboard and my previous room, there was no sign of it.

It was worth a trip back to the Metropolitan to see if I'd left it there; the proprietor greeted me like a long-lost cousin, but couldn't find it. Upset at losing my comfy sleeping bag that squashed up incredibly small and only weighed a kilo, I had to accept that the loss was probably due to my carelessness rather than theft.

Before the trip I'd wondered what backpackers did about their belongings in hostels, and had learnt that basically there was little choice but to trust your fellow travellers who, after all, were in the same position. My valuables – money, passport, tickets, cameras and Bruce – never left my person: they were either in my day bag or money belt and I slept with these beside my head. The rest of my belongings were left in the room when I went out. Who would want my dirty washing, unused water purification kit and grubby flip-flops? The only backpacker I met who'd had her whole pack stolen was an American and, ironically, despite all the dire warnings I'd been given about theft in Asia and South America, this was in New Zealand.

My first loss, Rachel's tape which I'd mislaid in Kathmandu, had been on quite an adventure of its own. Tour leader Carol had emailed to say that she'd found it under the bed when she returned to the hotel in Kathmandu six weeks later, a minor miracle that didn't say much for the cleaning in the hotel, and it had gone back to England with a member of that tour. In a few weeks I would get to read the little note Rachel had put inside the cover, but I could have done with it right now after a lonely week in Argentina.

Would I find warmth, either human or polyester, in Chile?

∞

On the flight from Buenos Aires to Santiago, I'd intended to study the guidebook to augment my knowledge of Chile, which was as thin as the country itself, but I was distracted by the peaks of the Andes thrusting themselves upward to join the aircraft above the solid layer of white cloud. Dark grey, with icy white slopes sliding into barren inaccessible valleys, they were startling, wild and forbidding.

Heading into Santiago, I had a distinct feeling of déjà vu as, arriving in another Catholic country on another Sunday, everything was shut. I wandered for hours down the wide, grid-planned streets, before arriving in the main square, the

Plaza de Armas, lined with churches and administrative buildings. Santiago was as incomprehensible as Buenos Aires. The locals – less European-looking than in Buenos Aires, shorter, darker with high cheekbones – strolled past in happy Sunday groups, talking in the same fast Spanish. Not all European visitors to the city had my difficulty in making contact with the locals, however; half the city had been named after Bernardo O'Higgins. Intrigued, I looked him up on the internet and discovered that he was the product of a liaison between the young daughter of a Chilean aristocratic and an Irish engineer. Bernardo was not only a republican hero who led the fight against Spanish domination but also proof that the Irish really do get everywhere.

I hadn't planned to stay in Santiago long but, anxious about how to travel in Peru, my next destination, I decided that for once some forward planning was needed. My now overpowering desire for company and conversation pointed me towards another tour. Also, third-hand stories among backpackers that Peru – and especially Lima – was awash with bandits and cut-throats were rife tipped the balance (even though not one of those backpackers had actually experienced any crime). After emailing tour companies telling my story and hoping for a discount, I hung around waiting for the replies.

∞

Staying in Santiago was no hardship as there were urgent tasks to attend to, such as buying a new sleeping bag and having a haircut – my resemblance to an Old English sheepdog was growing by the day. Also, Chileans like their coffee shops and ice-cream parlours even more than the Argentines, so it was pleasant to sit and people-watch when my feet ached.

On the day I'd allotted to shopping, it seemed odd that I was the only person waiting for the Subte to the modern shopping area of Providencia. When an empty ghost train drew up I became very twitchy, wondering if the people of Santiago knew something I didn't. Emerging into daylight, the streets were as deserted as Oxford Street on Christmas morning, the shops all shuttered. Wondering if Chile had slipped in another Sunday midweek, I checked my little pocket calendar and discovered it was May 1st, a public holiday. It was a far more reassuring reason than my imagined scenarios of escaped gas or alien invasions.

I needed a change of plan and, although Santiago was mostly a very flat city, it had two rocky hills protruding though its middle that seemed to be the only entertainment on offer. First I walked the up the Cerro Santa Lucia, a huge conical rock in the middle of the city, the views over the sprawling urban mass with the backdrop of the Andes making the steep climb worthwhile. Moving on to an even bigger rock, the Cerro San Cristobal which forms part of the large Parque Metropolitano, I took the funicular railway up the nearly vertical rock face.

At the top amidst well-tended terraced gardens, a 300-metre white statue of the Virgin Mary, surrounded by a collection of equally tall radio masts, watched over the city. Standing in solitary splendour, she looked as alien and isolated as I felt, and I wondered if she understood Spanish any better than me. Maybe the radio masts translated all the Spanish secrets from the city below. Coming down by cable car was fun but the journey ended in a part of the city I didn't recognise, and it was another long walk back to the centre.

Footsore, I took refuge in an internet café to study the responses to my emails. Obviously any tour had to include Machu Picchu, but all the web data about Peru insisted that I must walk the Inca Trail. There was a very generous offer from a tour company for a free trip walking the trail in my inbox. However, after five months I reluctantly had to acknowledge to myself that, although I felt lean and fit and, for the first time since 1972, had a flat stomach, weariness dogged my newly firm flesh.

If two days of walking round the city had made my legs ache, did I want four days of hard mountain walking and rough camping? Could I come this far and not do the Inca

Trail, to miss walking into Machu Picchu through the Sun Gate at dawn? But I imagined the humiliation as super-fit youngsters had to wait while a wheezing old-timer caught up and, even worse, the sound of my snoring echoing round the mountains.

∞

Leaving the decision for another day, I returned to do the shopping that I'd neglected the day before. Soon bored with looking at sleeping bags, none of which folded up smaller than a king-size quilt, I wandered into a smart hairdresser's where stylists dressed in chic black attended to customers hanging over black marble sinks. Struggling to communicate that I only wanted a trim, a head resembling an electrocuted hedgehog popped out from under a drier to clarify my request to the baffled assistant.

'Little – poco,' it said cheerily.

'Si, bueno,' the assistant beamed, proceeding to clip off the offending straggles. As I watched my hair being tidied up, a weather-beaten visage peered back from the mirror. Was that me? I smiled to see if the face responded and, sure enough, it grinned back. The stylist looked worried as I sat re-familiarising myself with my face.

It was now decision time. After much soul-searching, I decided not to walk the trail, opting instead for a ten-day Tucan Tour which started in Lima, went to Machu Picchu by train and finished in La Paz, Bolivia. Although it was a sensible decision, I already knew that back home, rested and refreshed, I would regret it.

∞

Now I could prepare to head up to the Atacama Desert on my way to Lima. Having spent most of the week in Santiago, my report, without the customary seven places visited in seven days to write about, had space to reflect that returning home was becoming a reality. I'd been surprised and even a bit embarrassed at how few homesick moments I'd suffered and how little I'd missed life back home. There were a few notable exceptions: my children, of course; real Cadbury's chocolate; mature cheddar cheese; my own bed; proper toilets, and flat, warm English beer. I even had dreams of lying in bed, nibbling cheese while downing pints of IPA, the brown nectar slipping down my throat.

Stronger than the anticipation of familiar home comforts was my dread of arriving back and picking up life exactly where I had left off. I knew this would probably happen but in my heart my secret dream was that I would be offered a job travel writing. Realistically, with thousands of wannabes out there, I knew that it wasn't very likely. This trip was a dream come true, so perhaps it was greedy to want another.

As well as my conviction that the Guardian was losing interest, Netjetter emails were also reducing. Whether this was because I was in a less well-travelled continent or, after five months everyone who wanted to say something had already said it, I didn't know. However, my musings on my imminent return struck a chord with my website audience and there was a surge of emails warning me of the likely difficulties. With four weeks left to enjoy, I didn't want to dwell on that. Bruce, who had secured quite a following of his own, received a flurry of emails about his photo with the leggy dancer.

∞

The pace of my travels picked up again as I flew north to Calama and took a minibus through the Atacama Desert, one of the driest areas in the world. At an altitude of 4,000 metres, this was an expanse of arid red desert covered in a white dusting that looked like snow but was in fact salt, with the red rock occasionally broken up by shallow pools of thick salty water or flat beds of dried salt cracked like crazy paving. To swap a busy city for this silent desert surrounded by snow-capped mountains and volcanoes was temporarily disorientating but, much as I enjoy wandering around cities, it was the discovery of strange areas like these that I really loved.

The small town of San Pedro de Atacama was the stuff that travel dreams are made of: sunshine, no traffic bar a couple of lethargic donkeys, few visitors and a sleepy peacefulness that unknotted the muscles and emptied the mind. Red dirt streets contrasted with low whitewashed stone houses topped with thatch or pantile roofs, and the bright sun shining in a deep blue cloudless sky lit up the snowy peaks of the surrounding mountains.

Equally captivating was the Residencial Sonchek, where a big, heavy wooden door led into a sun-baked, cobbled courtyard lined with a few rooms and a dormitory, each room with a little porch and straw roof. Past the jumble of shower, kitchen and wash rooms was a passage leading through to a small restaurant, where I had lunch in the sun with a chequered tablecloth and straw parasol.

The otherworldly feeling continued into the afternoon when I joined a bus trip out to the Valle de la Luna, a nature reserve with craters and rocks eroded into strange shapes by the wind. The desert is rich in minerals, particularly saltpetre, and a wealth of copper, lithium, borax and iodine, facts that don't mean much to the unscientific but apparently accounted for the multi-coloured layers that decorated the wind-eroded hills and rocks. One rock formation was called Tres Marias but I didn't understand why; another bore a distinct resemblance to ET.

The bus stopped at a sand dune as big as Ayers Rock, which we were meant to climb to see the sunset over the desert. The rarefied air and long day of travelling had exhausted me and I got only halfway before giving up and sitting on a rock to watch half the sunset.

This was my first night back in a dorm and I chose the bed farthest away from the only other occupant, a young Israeli man. Very tired, I immediately fell into a deep, dreamless sleep. Although I was up early to go on a day trip, the Israeli had already gone; whether my snoring drove him out will forever remain a mystery.

∞

At 5am the ten passengers – a mixture of French, Spanish, Swiss and Argentine, with me as the lone English person once again – climbed aboard the 4x4 minibus.

'¿Hola, habla Inglés?' I'd got this off pat now but was taken aback when the very handsome guide answered 'yes' in impeccable English. I was excited that, for once, I would know what was going on. We were driven out to a lake called Chaxa, famed for its rare flamingos; at dawn the lake features thousands of this particular black-tailed breed which can survive the altitude and the salt. On this day, like the bats of Mulu in Sarawak, the flamingos let me down. Only a few braved the cold morning air and stayed so far away that they were no more than black and pink dots balancing on needles.

We drove up and up into the mountains along steep, winding stony tracks, with not another human or motor in sight. Stopping in an area with an abundance of cacti and bushy plants, our excellent guide pointed out which ones could provide food or moisture in this barren waste. The prickliest was a plant called mother-in-law's tongue, which had little edible pods hidden amongst vicious spikes. We were warned not to drink the water here as it contains very high levels of arsenic, although for reasons that baffled the scientists, the indigenous population escape poisoning.

After yet more rocking and rolling up the steep slopes, we reached two vivid blue lakes, the Miscanti and Miniques, at the base of a beautiful snow-capped volcano. We could either walk from one lake to the other along the flat path of the valley or climb over the hill in between, which had panoramic views over both lakes. Most chose the hill, but at 4,500 metres, I was gasping for breath even when I walked very slowly. The rarefied air was like a scouring pad in my nose that solidified into cement when it reached my lungs. Vowing that I really, really, really would give up smoking if I survived the day, I descended to the lower lakeside path, desperate for air.

Our last stop was at the village of Toconao nestling in a valley full of trees and colourful plants that appeared out of the desert like a mirage. The houses and eighteenth-century church, built from white volcanic stone, bordered a tree-lined plaza. In the one little tourist shop I bought my very first present, a wall hanging with a llama design, blissfully unaware of how many of these I was to see over the coming weeks.

That evening, for the first time in what seemed months, I had company for dinner as five of the passengers ate together: two Frenchmen, who were researching starting a business hiring out motor caravans, an Austrian woman who did something diplomatic in Dubai and a teacher from Spain.

'Préférez-vous vin rouge ou le vin blanc?' asked a Frenchman.

'Rouge, por favor,' I replied, the effort of distinguishing schoolgirl French from sparse Spanish proving too much in the rarefied air. When the others had finished laughing, the Austrian took on the role of translator for the group, switching effortlessly between Spanish, English and French. A delicious meal of kebabs, with local musicians playing, a roaring fire and a light dusting of snow, made it an enjoyable evening, a welcome change from single meals in city restaurants.

∞

Time was short to reach Lima for the start of the Tucan Tour, and the long journey began inauspiciously as the lack of a lavatory at the bus station forced me to cross my legs for the first two hours to Calama. One of the problems with deserts is the absence of convenient bushes.

After a three-hour wait at Calama bus station, I boarded a coach for the eight-hour overnight journey to Arica. It came as no surprise that I was the only non-South American passenger. The idea of spending the night in a bus full of Chileans was daunting but at least my Spanish was improving and I could now ask for the essentials such as the toilet, a beer, water and a room.

Despite my linguistic improvement, I couldn't understand why the ticket man kept shouting at me but, after ten minutes of mutual exasperation it became apparent that the tickets had numbers and I was in the wrong seat. Despite moving to my better seat at the front, the shouting continued as he patted the empty seat beside me. Smiling and nodding as if I understood perfectly, I vowed never to speak to foreigners as if they were deaf.

After a few hours the ticket man sat beside me, indicating that this was where he was going to sleep – obviously what he had been trying to tell me earlier – but after ten minutes he got up and settled next to the burly man in the seat across the aisle. I was awake so it couldn't have been my snoring that drove him off, which left me wondering if nearly twenty-four hours of not off taking my boots or cleaning my teeth had anything to do with his move.

∞

The bus arrived at the station near Arica in the early morning and my next challenge was to cross into Peru. The guidebook suggested that there were collectivos to take you over the border, but what was a collectivo and what did it look like? Taxi drivers clamoured for my business but I shrugged them off as I looked for the elusive collectivo. I asked a man at a counter in the bus station and he pointed down the road. As I struggled along with the monster bag, a taxi driver came up to me.

'English? I have English!' he exclaimed, leading me towards his banana-coloured car, where an English couple was already ensconced. Apparently collectivos were nothing more exotic than taxis that collect a full load before setting off. When I reached the young couple, I launched into a torrent of English.

'Hello, my name's Sue. Where have you come from? Have you been to the Atacama? Fantastic, isn't it? I've been travelling for five-and-a-half months now...'

When they finally got a word in edgeways, the couple introduced themselves as Peter and Kath and told me they'd been travelling round Chile for three weeks and were about to go home.

'You're not involved in cake decorating, are you?' was my

final question.

'No,' replied Peter, giving me a strange look. 'I think we all need some strong coffee.'

The driver collected our passports and went to sort out the paperwork, part of the collectivo service apparently, and the English remained with the car and bags, taking it in turns to fetch coffee. Our affable and friendly driver decided that we three were enough to fill his taxi and drove off once the border was open. Several showings of documents later, we were in Peru and on our way to Tacna airport. It was strange how the last few weeks had transformed the tour buses of Australia into a fond memory.

11

Inca Tales

Weary and lonely after eighteen hours travelling, I entered Peru. My flight to Lima would not leave for nine hours and, as the guidebook didn't have much to say about the border town of Tacna, my first stop was the airline office to book an earlier flight. There wasn't one so I now had time to kill and, after two days on the road, the hottest feet and the smelliest breath in town.

Tacna was a busy town with a flourishing cross-border trade and an imposing cathedral, designed by the famous Mr Eiffel. After resting for an hour in a peaceful plaza shaded by huge palms, I needed to pee. So began a sequence of events that passed most of the day: need lavatory, find reasonable looking café, order drink, use lavatory, have drink, walk about a bit, need lavatory, find café.

Sometime in the morning I realised that my jacket was no longer with me. After an anxious retracing of footsteps and cafés, it was retrieved from the staff of a patisserie where I'd enjoyed a coffee, a cream cake and a pee. During a groundhog moment in the afternoon it went missing again and this time retrieved from the restaurant where I'd enjoyed soup and a pee. Thirty hours without sleep or a wash were beginning to take their toll; I decided I would be safest at the airport before anything vital was lost.

After a two-hour flight to Lima, a hotel car whisked me through seedy and industrial roads of Lima and reached the hotel at 11pm. Fit to burst after weeks of storing conversation,

I was thwarted as the Tucan Tour party had gone out, so I waited in the bar with a beer. A note informed me that I was booked onto the 7.30am flight to Cusco the next morning and the driver would pick me up at 4.30am, with the others following on a later flight. Was this my penalty for booking so late? Eking out my beer at one sip a minute, an hour and an empty glass later there was still no sign of any Tucan tourists. As the bar and my eyelids were about to close, I headed to my room and fell into bed.

∞

I was awake again at 3am the next morning for my dawn flight but the early morning shower had little impact on my brain, fuddled by only three hours sleep. I staggered down to the foyer, glad to be gone before the residue of grime in the shower tray was discovered.

On board a plane that would easily win the round-the-world prize for the least legroom, I found myself sitting with a party of forty Mormons from the US. An enormous and very panicky flier sat next to me, who frequently turned to his friend behind. 'Hey George, I don't think that wing flap's closed right up.'

Despite reassurance that the flap on the opposite wing was exactly the same, it wasn't long before he turned again. 'George, do yer hear that noise? I don't think the wheels have come up neat.'

His paranoia would have been amusing if it hadn't been for the fact that every time he turned, a mountain of flesh twisted my way, squashing me up against the window. We were both relieved when the plane landed safely in Cusco.

Whether it was her real name or a company requirement that employees must adopt a pseudonym from the animal kingdom, the young Peruvian Tucan rep who met me was called Gekko. At the hotel she offered me coca tea for the altitude and insisted that I rest for a couple of hours. I hadn't suffered from altitude sickness so far but the tea was delicious. For centuries the Indian population have kept a wad of the leaves of the coca plant in their cheeks as an appetite suppressant and mild stimulant, but today a much more profitable use is to process the leaves into cocaine.

After my nap, Gekko and I strolled round Cusco. Until now, South America had felt like an exotic version of Spain but here, in what the Incas called the 'navel of the world', I began to get a real sense of a different continent, still Spanish-influenced but with the unique native Indian heritage intertwined. In the large attractive main square, the Plaza de Armas, two flags fluttered from twin poles, the Peruvian flag and the rainbow flag of Tahuantinsuyo, symbolising the four regions of the old Inca Empire. One end of the square was dominated by the Catedral, whose huge twin towers of crumbling brown brick cast long shadows over the cobbled plaza; at the other was the ornate La Compania de Jesus church, built by the Jesuits. One side of the square was lined by the long, balconied facade of the Mercado Indigeno, a colourful sequence of shop windows displaying woven textiles, cheap panpipes and cuddly llama toys. Leading off from the plaza were steep cobbled streets of whitewashed houses; everywhere there were the remains of Inca walls, the smooth, dark irregularly shaped stone left unpainted.

After climbing a few of the cobbled lanes, I sat on a green bench on one of the triangles of grass and flowers that dotted the plaza, watching the teeming life of Cusco. The locals sat chatting or eating their lunch but the tourists were usually surrounded by young lads with packs of tacky postcards, shoeshine boys and Quechua-speaking indigenas, women and girls selling lottery tickets and assorted Peruvian knick-knacks. The women were dressed in traditional costumes: flared wool skirts with patterned borders, bright woven stripy shawls and hats of shapes ranging from fringed lampshades to small sombreros. Some were charging a few sol to be photographed with their children, and I willingly paid up for a shot of a group that included a very shaggy pet llama. At first I assumed the clothes were for the benefit of tourists, but soon understood that many Peruvians wore this attire everywhere and every day. As well as being attractive, it was warm and functional; I saw shawls serving as coat, baby carrier and shopping basket – sometimes all at once.

In the afternoon I was joined by my fellow Tucans, who turned out to number only two: Barry, a young, fit twenty-eight-year-old, and Dave in his early forties, gaunt and pale with the pallor of a Londoner who hasn't been outside for a year. The rest of the group had already been walking the Inca Trail for three days.

We joined an afternoon city coach tour that took us to the ornate Cusco Cathedral, most of which was shut off for restoration work, and the Coricancha, the Temple of the Sun, where simple Inca stone buildings had been excavated and restored to demonstrate the engineering genius of these people. The large stones fitted together perfectly without mortar, and had been fixed by a system of pegs that left no hint of a gap. During quakes they remained steadfast while the later Spanish buildings crumpled around and on top of them.

Barry's eyes lit up when we heard that 'sexywoman' was next, but much to his disappointment we turned up at Sacsayhuaman, the ruins of what is believed to have been a sanctuary and temple to the sun. Llamas with little heads bobbing on top of thick furry necks roamed beside the giant walls, a jigsaw of huge blocks of stone, some weighing up to a hundred tonnes. At our last stop, Tambomachay, or El Bano del Inca, a sacred spring spurted out from rock walls into a carved stone bath.

I had a captive audience to satiate my need for English conversation and Dave, Barry and I chatted late into the evening.

'What do you do when you're not exploring Peru?' I asked Dave.

'I work in London for the Department of Education,' he answered.

'I work in Education Welfare.'

'Oh, I've been researching you lot. I've been working on

182

Tackling Truancy Together.'

'I know it,' I said. 'It makes an excellent doorstop.'

'I'm in railway design,' said Barry.

'You design trains?'

'Actually, no, I study the space of the aisles. It's quite complicated to leave room for trolleys.'

At that, we agreed it was time for bed and that Peru was much more exciting than our jobs back home.

∞

The big day arrived – we were going to Machu Picchu, not on foot but in a bright yellow-and-red steam engine that was besieged by colourful vendors of rainbow-hued clothes and trinkets. After Barry, who had been studying the ancient couplings between the carriages, was dragged onto the train, we sat back to enjoy the three-and-a-half-hour journey.

The train climbed the steep slopes out of Cusco in a series of zig-zags, at times in reverse, which had Barry in a frenzy of excitement. After a gentle descent to Ollantaytambo, the train wound its way through a narrow gorge where the water of the Urubamba River frothed over rapids and the hills rose sheer and wild on either side. A group of trekkers on the same train grew more and more excited as we neared Km 88, the start of the Inca Trail, and they heaved their packs onto their backs when the train stopped at a crossing. The slope upwards from the crossing looked very steep and I regretted not being younger and fitter.

Aguas Calientes was at the end of the line, where the track served as the high street, bisecting the bustling market where we had to fight our way through the stalls of Peruvian fabrics and the hawkers with their strips of postcards of Machu Picchu. A steep walk out of the station led to the bus, which navigated the tall, pointed mountains in a series of hairpin bends. After a few miles among these dramatic mountains, it was clear why the Spanish conquerors never found this Inca city and how it remained undiscovered until 1911. How could a city have been built in such an inaccessible place?

I felt nervous approaching the entrance to the city, wondering if I would be impressed, as with the Taj Mahal, or disappointed, as at Ayers Rock. That's the trouble with iconic places: they have much to live up to. Once through the entrance gate, every inch had been used either for garden terraces or buildings and plazas that cascaded down the hillside. In contrast, empty, pointed craggy mountains, dark grey apart from braids of greenery that clung to their slopes, surrounded it, their tops hidden in the clouds.

I breathed a sigh of relief – it was spectacular. Gekko, with obvious pride at her ancestors' achievement, led us round the maze of green plazas and through the shells of a multitude of buildings connected by walled alleys and more than a hundred stairways.

'Choose your bath tub,' she joked as we climbed the flight of stairs beside a series of sixteen ceremonial baths, where small waterfalls filled carved stone basins. To the left was El Torreón, the round Temple of the Sun built on a huge rock, the walls as smooth as glass with few joints between the enormous blocks of granite. In a cave underneath was an altar, the Royal Tomb, where mummies were discovered. Next door was El Palacio de la Ñusta, or the Palace of the Princesses.

'About eighty per cent of the skeletons found in Machu Picchu were of women,' explained Gekko, 'so it might have been home to priestesses.'

I tried to imagine living up here in a predominantly female commune. There was water and well-cultivated land but at 2,400 metres it must have been bitterly cold in winter. It had been an arduous enough journey to get here by train and bus; in Inca times, once you were here it would have been virtually impossible to leave if you decided the priestesshood wasn't for you after all.

Walking upward, we came to the Sacred Plaza. On the far side there was a stone platform that looked out to the Cordillera Vilcabamba mountain range ahead and the sheer drop to the Rio Urubamba below. Surveying the inaccessible land above, below and all around, I was struck again by the incongruity of the location. There were important temples on the other three sides of the plaza, the most striking being the Temple of the Three Windows, which overlooked the city below. The stones of the wall of the Principal Temple were taller than me; running my hands over the smooth cold stone, I couldn't feel the joins between them.

Up another steep path was the Intihuatana, the 'hitching post of the sun', a rock pillar used as a calendar. Sculpted out of the rock itself, a rectangular post set in a smooth slab had been used by Inca astronomers to predict the solstices.

Left to wander alone, I crossed the grassy central plaza to make my way through the more mundane living quarters and Artisans' Quarter, where there was a large rock carved into the head of a condor, sacred to the Incas. The surrounding boulders formed its body. Sitting on the grass for a rest, I watched the cloud begin to descend and had another of my 'what a lucky sod I am' moments. The weather had been good, with none of the low cloud that often shrouded the site, and there were relatively few visitors as it was a month before the tourist season began in earnest. Most of all, I felt grateful for the opportunity to be there at all, as faraway Peru had been high on my wish list but near the bottom in terms of affordability. In a dreamy reverie, I felt uniquely close to the sky; the sheer abundance of abandoned ruins gave Machu Picchu an ethereal, almost ghostly atmosphere.

It began to rain as we went for lunch and stopped just as we were deciding what to do with the remaining few hours. Barry wanted to climb Huayna Picchu, the impossibly steep-sided mountain facing Macchu Picchu, which looked to me as though it could be tackled only with a team of sherpas and miles of climbing rope. Dave, whose face had turned a shade paler as he looked at the mountain, gallantly offered to keep me company on a walk to the Sun Gate, an hour away along a narrow path snaking round the side of the mountain.

At the Gate, a group of exhausted walkers was resting after completing the Inca Trail. It was clear from their faces that they would boast of this achievement for the rest of their lives. Looking back over the distant view of Machu Picchu tucked in amongst the towering mountains, I felt a pang of regret that this wasn't the way I'd arrived at the city.

As the last bus back to Aguas Calientes zigzagged its way down the mountain, a young boy in Inca dress ran the quick route – straight down, stopping whenever he crossed the road to wave. Each time we turned a sharp bend I looked for him; he didn't miss one, arriving at the bottom hardly out of breath and hopping on the bus to claim his reward. May an Inca curse strike the miserable skinflints who didn't tip him.

On the train, we joined up with the rest of the tour who'd walked the trail. Though a tired, grubby bunch, a few ill with colds and tummy troubles, they had that same buzz and sense of achievement as the group at the Sun Gate.

'Jesus, I smell!'

'I hope I never have to do another crap behind a rock.'

'After sharing a tent with you, I rename you Inca stinker.'

'I'll never forget that climb at the Dead Woman's Pass.'

'All worth it in the end, though,' said the tour leader to unanimous agreement.

On the train and back at the hotel, where the others prioritised laundry, showers and bed, Barry, Dave and I felt very clean, fresh and left out.

∞

The next day featured a bus tour to the Sacred Valley to see two Inca fortresses, Pisac and Ollantaytambo, the latter being where the Spanish Conquistadors suffered one of their few defeats in battle. This wasn't such a surprise if you considered that the Spanish soldiers, like us, probably had no breath or energy left after climbing the steep stone terracing up to the temple at the top of the hill.

Arriving at the colourful market of Pisco, the realisation that I only had a couple of weeks left precipitated some serious present buying. The choice was overwhelming: decorated pottery, embroidered clothes, wall hangings galore, alpaca knitwear, jewellery, and all in vibrant local colours.

At the thought of returning to work soon after my return home, I considered a new career as an entrepreneur, emptying my big bag and filling it with Peruvian artefacts to sell in Cambridge. I pictured myself standing in the middle of King's Parade dressed in a poncho and waving panpipes at passing American tourists. The alpaca jumpers here were selling for about $5, and could be sold for ten times as much at home. I scribbled some sums on the back of an envelope but came to the conclusion that I would have to sell at least three thousand jumpers to cover my bank loan, and another five hundred woolly hats to take care of the interest. Oh well, it was a nice thought for five minutes.

Back in Cusco, I had to miss most of the drinking session in the Irish bar in order to write my report, as we were off to the Amazon jungle in the morning. This is the biggest and least populated rainforest, covering half of Peru but containing only five per cent of its population, according to the guidebook. It was to be my seventh rainforest and sadly, my last. I remembered my solemn promise to the travel nurse not to go to the Amazon as I didn't have the correct anti-malaria tablets for that area, but with nothing to suggest that Peruvian mosquitoes would find me any tastier than Asian ones, I was prepared to risk it.

∞

After an early start to catch the tiny plane to fly east to the Amazon Basin, we landed in Puerto Maldonado, once a logging port but long denuded of trees, and now a centre for gold and oil prospectors. A three-hour boat trip up the Tambopata River took us into the Zona Reservada Tambopata-Candamo, a protected area of primary rainforest, and to our base at the Tambopata Jungle Lodge. As the crisp, dry air of the mountains changed to the soggy rainforest heat, I welcomed the familiar humidity as it wrapped itself around me like a comfort blanket. The camp was a collection of thatched huts with one large communal wooden building for eating and recreation. There was no electricity on site but the three-bed huts did have a cold shower and a sit-down toilet. I was the first to christen the one in my hut – with my book accidentally dropping into the basin, luckily before I'd taken a seat. Anxious to know the ending, I fished it out and hung it up to dry.

It started raining when we arrived and didn't stop for the next forty-eight hours, so our afternoon walk to a forest farm in a clearing hacked out of the jungle was a rather damp affair. An extended clan of several adults, with the dark skin and sleek black hair of the local population, and numerous wide-eyed, scantily clad children with snotty noses, farmed fruit here in the forest. Avocados the size of melons, oranges the size of grapefruit, massive mangoes, lemons, star fruit and pineapples hung off trees; there were enough lying on the ground for us to slip an avocado or two into our bags without guilt. Joselin, our young Bolivian guide, proudly showed us the new mahogany and other hardwood trees that had been planted among the fruit trees as part of a government scheme to sustain the ecology of the rainforest.

After our candlelit evening meal, Joselin suggested we go caiman-spotting. After finding out that caiman were alligators rather than illegal loggers, I signed up. Only five of us volunteered for the trip, which had us slipping through the mud to the water's edge by torchlight, clambering into a wet canoe and then being rowed through pitch-black water while the riverbank was swept with a searchlight. Our reward for sitting in silence for an hour in the pouring rain, with the searchlight acting as a magnet for every insect for miles, was the sight of one pair of eyes sticking out of the water like two ping-pong balls. At least I could claim sight of part of an Amazon alligator, if not a whole one.

Worried by the return of a cold, I told my hut companions to throw something at me if I snored. In the morning, having felt a couple of thuds in the night and seeing the sullen face of the light-sleeping American in the next bed, I feared the worst. I wasn't solely to blame for her sleepless night, as someone in the adjoining hut had a bad cough.

The rain continued all night and there wasn't much sign of it letting up that day so after breakfast we squelched our way to a long line of wellington boots to prepare for a 14km hike through the rainforest. The American opted to stay behind to sleep. Delayed by that seductive second cup of coffee, I arrived late to find only a heap of mismatched boots fit for one-legged giants or class of four-year olds. My leaky walking boots would have to do.

I was acutely aware that this was the last time I would feel the excitement of trekking through rainforest, but this was the first time I'd done so in continuous rain. Here again were the familiar smells of earth and rotting vegetation, the innumerable shades of green, the artistic shapes of tree roots, the tangled vines, the insects whining and humming – oh, how I loved it. Despite plodding through ankle-high mud, crossing streams via slippery logs, and being whipped by dripping leaves and branches, the whole group was in high spirits. Joselin showed us a 'walking' bamboo that shoots out one large root and over time grows from this root, thus gradually 'walking' through the forest. Another plant that caused coarse jokes was the labia rosa, whose flower resembles big red lips. However, with twenty of us crashing through the undergrowth, we didn't see much wildlife apart from one of the foot-high giant snails that inhabit this area and a hoatzin, a huge prehistoric-looking bird with a spiky punk hairdo that flew overhead, known locally as 'stinky bird'.

We stopped by a lake for lunch and the rain eased for an hour. The lake, surrounded by tall trees, ferns and creepers, looked empty and quiet, but beneath the surface were shoals of piranhas. Joselin disappeared for a while and came back, in true Blue Peter style, with a collection of sticks, each sporting a line and hook on the end, and pots of scraps of raw meat. Continuing in this DIY fashion, two punts half-submerged beside the lake had to be bailed out before we could go out onto the lake to fish.

I'd always imagined piranhas to be huge with jagged teeth, not the little sprats that surfaced to look at us. What they lacked in size, they made up for in speed and our simple rods and lines were no match for these crafty beggars as they swam rings round us, snatching the bait before we could blink. It became a group obsession to catch at least one and we concentrated hard on trying to strike before the bait was gone. A couple of the men stayed in the boats throughout lunch, determined not to be beaten, but at the end of the contest the score remained Tucan-fishers nil, Piranhas one hundred.

Making our way back, I felt sad that it was my last rainforest day. Before the trip, I'd been aware of news items and nature programmes about the loss of this vital part of the planet's ecosystem, but they hardly seemed real. Now I'd explored it, witnessed its richness, smelt it, breathed it and touched it, I knew that it would be personal from now on.

Back at the camp, a cold shower had little appeal, so it was a swift change into dry clothes and over to the recreation hut. My boots were as wet on the inside as they were muddy on the outside and my very last Malaysian toilet roll was pressed into service as stuffing to absorb the moisture, leaving me with flip-flops to wear until the morning. We had yet another candlelit evening in the camp and played a card game with the dubious name of 'Arsehole', an offering from the Australian contingent that involved raucous abuse of the unfortunate person who couldn't follow suit and therefore picked up the pile of discards.

After a short night's sleep, we were up at 3.30am for the three-hour boat journey back to Puerto Maldonado in the rain. It was a very wet, cold, muddy and tired group that boarded the plane for Cusco.

∞

Our enterprising tour leader solved the problem of the snorer (me, of course) and the cougher (Jenny from New Zealand) by allocating us the same room. I'd blocked out the memory of the relentless pace of tours and the early mornings, but it was vividly brought home to me by a 6am call to board the minibus for a nine-hour journey to Puno on the edge of Lake

Titicaca.

The road climbed up over a mountain pass and onto the altiplano, the high plain that extends into Bolivia, where herds of alpaca and llamas roam the bare landscape. In the little Peruvian villages, the local people were dressed in colourful traditional clothing; there wasn't a scrap of denim or PVC to be seen, and the women all sported little bowler hats perched on the tops of their heads, looking like hippies at a Laurel and Hardy convention.

Like the rest of Peru, the towns and villages that we passed through were full of unfinished buildings; taxes were levied only when the roof was put on, so few buildings had more than a few rows of bricks to the second storey. Apparently, to have an upper storey was quite a status symbol, indicating that you were doing very well for yourself.

In the centre of the altiplano is Lake Titicaca, more than 170kms long and 60kms wide. In Puno, the sight of a harbour and the blue water stretching to the horizon made it seem like a sea rather than a lake, but the distant Cordillera Real, with its mountain tops covered in snow and, of course, the thin air, testified to every one of its 3,820 metres above sea level.

After a night in Puno we clambered into a motorised boat on the dark blue water to visit the reed beds that grow a couple of hours away on the lake. Here the Uros people, an independent native tribe, live on floating islands made from a metre-thick layer of the plant. The reeds gradually rot from the bottom and the islands are renewed by placing fresh ones on top. The people had taken to the water many centuries before to evade the Incas and other dominant tribes but had intermarried, so there were no pure Uros left. They used to live by fishing and trapping birds but tourism became a big source of income, although visitors are allowed onto only three or four of the eighty islands.

At the sight of our boat, the islanders laid out their wares of woven wall-hangings and miniature reed boats; jostling children lined up to accompany us round the houses, which had been turned into little museums with stuffed birds and more replica reed boats. Full-sized totora reed canoes, that could hold ten passengers, were ready to take us on a trip around the island. The expressions on the faces of the islanders, turned almost black by exposure to the elements, told a story of resignation, boredom and a desperation to sell something.

Although I had my ride in a reed boat and bought a wall hanging from a woman sitting on the reeds, I didn't like being on the islands. As I squelched about, the smell of decomposing vegetation and the abundance of flies made me feel unwell. Like many ethnic attractions, this seemed like a commercial complex to milk tourists – an Arndale of the Lake – and I wondered how much of the islanders' traditional way of life remained in the face of tourists' fascination with their watery world. I felt guilty to be there, intruding on – and thereby changing – a unique way of life. I wondered whether the cold winter brought relief or hardship with the loss of income.

After another three hours on the lake, we landed on the island of Amantani where we were to spend the night. Lydia, the shy eldest daughter of our host family, led Jenny and me up a very steep hill to her house, smiling at our slow progress at this altitude. The local families take it in turns to host the visitors; we were a source of extra income for the islanders that didn't seem to interfere with their normal way of life. It was like stepping back in time: no electricity or piped water, no crime, no vehicles and therefore no roads. The islanders lived by selling woven goods, fishing and farming, mostly growing potatoes and the local grain. The government had built a hospital on the island but nobody used it, preferring to rely on the local expertise and herbal medicines, and the islanders all looked healthy enough.

Lydia's stone house had only two rooms: guests upstairs and the family – parents and five children – below. The kitchen, with a stick fire, was built on the side and the 'bathroom' was a hut fifty metres away containing a couple of planks over a deep hole in the ground. The islanders spoke Quechua but understood Spanish, which was fine if you could speak Spanish, but neither Jenny or I had more than a few stock phrases, so we communicated by sign language.

A few brave males from our group were tempted into a game of football with the local lads in the village square, but after ten minutes the square resembled chucking-out time in a town centre at the weekend. The normally fit young men staggering on rubbery legs, their faces white as they gasped for breath. No wonder the football teams of this area invariably won at home.

Once they'd recovered, we all walked very slowly up to Pachamama (Mother Earth), the pre-Inca ruins at the top of the hill, followed the whole way by a young boy playing his panpipes. This could have been a romantic accompaniment to the walk if he'd been able to play anything other than Frère Jacques; by the time we reached the top, we were ready to ding his dong up his dang. We were rewarded at the summit with spectacular views of the terraced hills of the island spilling down to the vast lake shore, with the mountains just visible on the horizon. As the sun set, the sweeping clouds acquired red linings and the dark of the rocks and islands were silhouetted against the purple water.

Back at our lodgings, after dinner had been brought to our room (predominately potatoes) and the temperature had plummeted, Jenny and I sat shivering over a candle wondering what we would do all evening. The problem was solved by Lydia and her mother, who appeared at the door with arms full of clothes. After a few minutes of gesticulating and tugging at our clothes, we realised that we were meant to put them on. We both opted to keep thermal leggings and T-shirts on as the two giggling women dressed us in three flouncy petticoats followed by blue wool skirts topped by beautiful white embroidered blouses. A wide multi-coloured woven band was tied around our waists, pulled so tightly that we both gasped, and the costume was finished off with a black woollen shawl decorated with intricate embroidery.

'Wow, look at us,' Jenny exclaimed.

Lydia and her mother led us down to the village hall for the dance and, when we saw that we were the only ones from our group in costume, we felt very special and beamed all evening. Others, not understanding what was happening, had declined the clothes.

The four local musicians in stripy ponchos, with a drum, a little guitar, flutes and panpipes, beat out the tunes while the villagers dragged us onto the dance floor. Though quite shy about dancing, the clothes gave me a confidence usually only achieved through alcohol, and I was soon tripping the light fantastic in walking boots. The dances were in big circles, always ending with a manic careering round the room that left me dizzy, breathless and hot. Jenny and I now understood how the locals kept warm and we regretted the thermals. There was beer for sale but the thought of having to venture out to the shed in the middle of the night made us all drink sparingly.

As I stood outside for a breath of fresh air, the only light came from the mass of brilliant stars overhead. I felt overwhelmed by a mix of contradictory emotions. This evening was very special, exciting and different, as was the island with no hotels, tourist shops, beggars or thieves. The people were genuinely friendly, and our stay felt like a shared experience to mutual benefit and enjoyment – tourism at its best.

Yet underneath there lurked a sadness that soon my adventure would be over. What then? With no more evenings like this, no more days wandering at leisure, no more mountains to climb, seas to cross, wouldn't life be unbearably mundane? I rejoined the dance, my step a little heavier.

Sleeping badly that night, freezing despite the thermals and five rough, woollen blankets, I wondered who was curled up in my long-lost cosy sleeping bag.

∞

Early next morning we waved goodbye to our hosts and Amantani. We stopped off at the neighbouring island of Taquile, a busier and more visited island two hours away. Entering the town from the landing jetty was like walking onto the set of a spaghetti Western; the footpath took us through a wide stone arch to a town square of red earth and whitewashed buildings.

While we enjoyed a much-anticipated, steaming hot coffee, the mayor and mayoress of the village came to talk to us via a local interpreter. They were handsome figures in their red and black clothes, the mayoress with even more petticoats than I'd worn the night before and the mayor with a knitted hat with ear-covers under his rakish black felt hat.

They sat shyly, sharing a Coke, while we learned how these leaders are chosen each year by all the islanders. Apparently the women hold sway and the men vote as their wives tell them (a system that seemed to have served the island well). Knitting is one of the main crafts on the island and the men walked around with needles clacking. At the cooperative shop that sold the island's high-quality woollen goods, Barry bought a tiny traditional Peruvian knitted hat with earflaps for Bruce.

I bought a friendship bracelet from one of the enterprising children for my friend Ann. She had presented me with one when I set off; it was still going strong, outlasting my 'Pushkar passport', the dyed string tied on by a holy man back in December. After I'd set off on my round-the-world adventure, Ann had finally packed a suitcase, a tent and her goldfish and, after years of idle threats, driven off to live in Ireland on an adventure of her own. Only the onset of winter and a mild case of trench foot finally drove her into respectable lodgings, where she had fallen for Michael O'Something, a silver-haired charmer.

My son Ben, too, had finally tired of resting and in March had gone to Japan to teach English for a year. It was uncomfortable to think that people at home were carrying on or radically changing their lives without me.

Roused from my nostalgia, I clambered back into the boat for the three-hour journey back to Puno. We exchanged books to pass the time and I tried not to look embarrassed as I swapped my battered, twenty-fourth-hand novel for a smart straight-from-the-airport book; I kept quiet about the jungle dunny-dunking. Thanks to the wonderful book-swap shops that had sprung up on backpacker routes, I'd never been short of something to read. You could swap any redundant guidebook for a relevant one, too.

This was our last night as a full group; half of us were heading back to Lima the next day and the rest carrying on to La Paz in Bolivia. After that initial bad meal, the steaks in South America had been fantastic, but the dish of the day at our farewell meal was guinea pig or cuy, a delicacy in Peru. Like chickens in the farmyards of Britain, these little rotund rat-like creatures roam the houses and yards of Peru, blissfully ignorant of their destiny. With a grandiose flourish the waiter set down the dish in the middle of the table.

'Cuy, muy bueno!' he announced.

Spread-eagled on the plate was a guinea pig, pegged out like a hide drying in the sun. Its skin had been roasted to golden-brown crackling, and its head was intact with little white teeth exposed in a last defiant sneer.

'Ugh, it's whole. I can't eat that,' squealed one of the girls.

'Looks delicious,' said a boy.

'How could you eat that poor little thing?' wailed a female vegetarian, her eyes filling with tears.

'Right, how many for the pig?' asked a drunken Australian, brandishing the carving knife.

As the controversy raged, I decided that the cooked cuy looked too much like Eugene and Marmalade, childhood pets, and I couldn't bring myself to violate it. Our stay in Peru ended with the bonds forged in the trials of the Inca Trail broken asunder by this little dead animal.

12

The End Is High

Bolivia hadn't been on my original itinerary so I was grateful that the tour led me into the highest and most isolated country in South America, even though it would be no more than a fleeting glimpse.

Once those heading back to Lima had departed, there were only ten of us left on the minibus that crossed the border into Bolivia and headed for La Paz. At first there seemed to be no obvious difference between Peru and Bolivia, as we drove around the same lake and the people wore the same colourful knitwear and bowler hats.

At Estrecho de Tiquina, an estuary of Lake Titicaca, the bus was loaded onto a raft, with a rickety motor boat for the passengers. As usual, the toilet was needed before the female contingent could contemplate being on water, and our search led us to a brick building built in the style of a pigsty, with low walls and short partitions between the holes in the ground.

It's surprising how quickly standards drop and tolerance levels rise. Though not fastidious, at home I wouldn't contemplate leaving the house for work or an evening out without a shower and change of clothes. During the preceding five months, such matters had become peripheral and my clothes had begun to develop a unique ecosystem to rival that of the rainforest. By the judicious use of panty liners, the life of underwear could be extended, and no one had been close enough to me to distinguish between dirt and suntan. After a while the toilets scarcely merited the raising of an eyebrow, although they still required a peg on the nose, and I was grateful for anything that had walls, even if they were only a metre high.

Reunited with our bus and turning inland from the lake, we climbed steeply to reach the high Altiplano, with the towering Andes just visible in the distance. This was a wide, desolate area of brown scrub, empty but for a few small villages and the occasional herd of alpaca escorted by a blanket-covered Bolivian.

In a state of lethargy induced by a flat road through barren landscape, we were jerked awake by the sudden appearance of El Alto, a town that looked as if all the rubbish, broken cars, scrap metal and ragged children of the continent had been swept up and dumped in a heap in it. The pot-holed streets, surrounded by ugly crumbling tenements, were peopled by hardy Andeans scraping a living from a chaotic jumble of stalls, recycling the already recycled.

As suddenly as it appeared, El Alto was gone and the earth in front of us dropped away to form a five-kilometre-wide canyon containing La Paz. It was as if thousands of tiny matchbox buildings had been poured into a huge sticky basin, attaching themselves to the sides. To look down on the city 400 metres below and up at the snow-capped peaks of Mount Illimani was a never-to-be-forgotten sight, and we were all wide awake and buzzing with excitement as the bus plunged down the steep road into the city.

Although the centre of La Paz is in a crater, it is still four kilometres above sea level. Walking from our hotel down the cobbled streets that led to the main thoroughfare was easy but walking back up was hard in such thin air. The streets were busy and so densely packed with stalls and street traders that I wondered how the shops survived, given that everything from shampoo to digital cameras was available on the pavement. Dense markets of fruit, vegetables and rainbow-coloured cloth filled the steep alleys off the main streets. Unlike Buenos Aires and Santiago, the people thronging the streets were predominantly Indian, many wearing the traditional costume of warm, colourful blankets and little hats.

In one of the city squares, the Plaza San Francisco, the stone steps of the Basilica were packed with a vocal but peaceful crowd waving trade union banners in a political demonstration. In this noisy, busy, colourful city everyone shouted, not only when selling their wares but also in normal conversation.

∞

The next day the tour disbanded, leaving only me, Barry and Damien, a young Australian, to join three hairy French hippies on a tour to Tiahuanaco, the site of the ceremonial centre of Bolivia's pre-Inca civilisation. The site is only partially excavated and the main structure, the Akapana Pyramid, was little more than a grassy hill, but all around were sunken courtyards and platforms with giant monoliths covered in hieroglyphics and intricate designs. Our guide was a young Bolivian woman who rushed us round the museum and the sights at breakneck speed.

'Keep up! Listen to what I am saying. Not a lot is known about this early empire but look, carved stones, ceramics, gigantic sandstone rocks come from forty kilometres away, so it was an advanced people.'

As we ran after her, she screeched to a halt.

'Empire, fifth century BC, used to cover Bolivia, Peru and parts of Chile and Argentina. Now questions, please.'

We stood silently, catching our breath while she admonished us. 'It is not good that you are not asking questions. There should be lots of questions.'

She marched off to the next monument while the French hippies made rude gestures behind her back that alluded to descent from a Nazi exile.

'Here, Puerta del Sol, gateway carved out of a single stone, weighs 44,000 kilograms. Take a photo!'

Two large monoliths, El Ponce and El Fraile, stood on guard at the temple sites, covered in intricate designs, with their hands holding carved tablets.

'Why is this one called a Ponce?' asked Barry, relieved to have thought of a question.

'Ponce was a famous Bolivian archaeologist. Well done!' Barry received a pat on the arm.

'Teacher's pet,' I whispered.

In one courtyard there was a wall with faces carved in relief. Some were worn away but one, sharply defined, showed a Chinese face which suggested contact with people on the other side of the world. Another with cheeks puffed out hinted at an early addiction to coca leaves. When a Frenchman put his hat on one of the stone heads for a photo, the guide's face turned purple.

'Forbidden! You are very bad, very bad.'

Back in La Paz, Damien headed off to Chile. Despite the fact he had a flight home at 4am the next morning, I persuaded Barry to go to a peña, a Bolivian folk music and dancing show. The long walk to the restaurant took us down narrow, dark alleys, and I was glad of the company of a strong young man.

Nervously I ordered an alpaca steak and watched anxiously to see if the waiter staggered in with a whole roasted animal on a platter. As only a chunk arrived and I've never owned a pet alpaca, I had no qualms in tucking into the delicious meat, which tasted like a cross between lamb and beef.

The music and dance were excellent, with various bands playing haunting Andean melodies and fast Spanish Lambada-type tunes on charangos (little guitars), pipes and quirquinchos (drums). The dancing was exciting; even Barry's feet tapped a sort of fandango as the dancers waved handkerchiefs. Of all the dance shows I'd seen so far, this was by far the best – and Barry didn't regret his lack of sleep.

∞

Having fulfilled my need for company with a ten-day tour, I was happy to return to wandering the streets of La Paz at my own slow pace. I fancied going to Rurrenabaque, a small town deep in the Western Amazon Basin that had come highly recommended by an emailer but, with so little time left, I reluctantly decided to venture only as far as Coroico in the Yungas, a fertile area of valleys and gorges that linked the high Andean altiplano and the Amazon basin.

With my limited command of the Spanish language, it was more by luck than skill that I managed to buy a ticket for the ten o'clock bus rather than one of the sacks of potatoes heaped beside the counter. In true Latin-American style, when there were enough burly Bolivians with their sacks of produce to fill the minibus, we left for Coroico at 11.30. The first hour was a picturesque drive in the mountains on a good paved road that climbed into the clouds and over La Cumbre pass at 4,725 metres, where the dark grey rock was peppered with a dusting of snow.

Once through the pass, the road divided and from there on it was in every sense downhill all the way as it degenerated into a dirt track hacked out of the side of the mountain. As the track was only one vehicle wide, if anything came the other way, one vehicle had to reverse to a location on the unprotected edge, where it was wide enough for the wheels to hover without going over. Waterfalls ran off the mountain, falling onto bus and road alike, turning the dirt into deep mud. I had the misfortune to be sitting on the side where, if I dared look, the edge of the path fell away in a sheer drop down the vertical side of the mountain.

The proliferation of little shrines bore witness to the fate of many travellers along this notorious road. A few years before, a one-way system had been introduced – mornings from La Paz to Coroico and afternoons in reverse – but, as convoys built up behind the slowest vehicles leading to reckless overtaking, the accident rate soared even higher. The system was abandoned.

At a point where the mixture of mud and water had produced a quagmire of deep waterlogged ruts, a digger sat serenely in the middle of the road, with no sign nearby of workmen, driver or any recent human activity. As we tried to manoeuvre round it, the agonised revving of the engine in my ears and a sheet of mud spray flying past the window made a translation of the driver's Spanish announcement unnecessary: we were stuck. To add to the pantomime, a lorry with a jocular band of men riding on top of the load appeared from the other direction, all the locals jeering loudly at our plight.

I followed the other passengers off the bus and plodded through the mud to a drier section further on. Eventually the bus was shaken free and it squeezed past the lorry, finally arriving at a point where we could get back on.

This road was truly scary and, for the first time since my ride into Mumbai, I felt I was in real danger. While contemplating the ease with which the bus could slip or slither over the edge, it occurred to me that Bruce was guarding my passport and other documents in La Paz. Again, there wasn't a soul in the world apart from the ticket seller at the bus station who knew I was here. With the thought of my crumpled body remaining unidentified and my children never knowing what fate had befallen me, I came out in a cold sweat. In a flash of inspiration, I remembered that I had a few Guardian Netjetter cards in my purse and surreptitiously slipped one into every pocket, confident that a national newspaper would be able to sort out the protocol and repatriate my body parts. Feeling a little better, I dared to look beyond the cliff edge to the stunning scenery: tall hills with rich jungle clinging to the steep sides and verdant valleys.

Shaken, mentally exhausted yet all in one piece, I arrived in the little town of Coroico, perched on the side of a hill at 1,760 metres. It was a pretty, sleepy place, with steep cobbled streets leading up from the central Plaza de Mayo, which had an array of little shops and cafes.

The hostel nestled at the top of a flight of stone steps, with a sun-baked café area and big rooms that led onto a patio with glorious views over the surrounding banana and coffee groves and the sweeping Yungas behind. After strolling around the village I sat on the patio, reading, sunning myself and taking in the views. The hostel had a swimming pool but it hadn't occurred to me to bring my costume half-way up a mountain. I was the only customer in the hostel restaurant that evening and when the waiter disappeared after bringing my meal, I ate in an overwhelming silence.

Back in my room, it was time for a shower but I noticed that the water heater was attached to the shower head, with bare wires connecting it to the electricity supply. As I turned it on, the lights dimmed and it gave out an increasingly distressed hum punctuated by the odd crackle. There was no way unearthed that I was going naked under that thing, so I decided to stick with the tanned look.

∞

In the morning, as I walked up an almost vertical hill, there didn't appear to be any other travellers around. I exchanged nods with a couple of village women. Though I'd not worried about walking alone before, my not very up-to-date guidebook did advise women against walking alone in this area, so at the edge of the village I reluctantly turned back and decided to return to La Paz.

Booking the last seat on the afternoon bus, I was surprised it was a window seat, but as soon as I sat down I knew why: all of the legroom was taken up by the wheel arch. When a rotund Bolivian with a big cardboard box sat next to me, I knew I was in trouble. With my knees under my chin, the holdall and day sack squashed above and below them, however I positioned myself different parts of me either went dead, locked themselves or went into spasm. The man beside me must have thought I had tics, either live or nerve-induced, as I jiggled and fidgeted for the whole journey. At least the road didn't seem quite so bad going back, partly as it was uphill and I was on the side that looked out onto the rising cliff face, but most of my attention was focused on trying to ease the pain in my body.

When we rejoined the main road, there was a much needed 'comfort stop', where my legs nearly buckled as feeling returned in the form of vicious pins and needles. As I emerged from the toilet, a barrage of shouts and horn blasts greeted me and I was taken aback that that I merited such a reception. In reality, my male travelling companions were impatient to get back to La Paz.

∞

It was time to start wending my way back to Peru, and I broke the bus journey to Puno with two nights at Copacabana, on the banks of Lake Titicaca. I stopped here mainly because the name was familiar from a song, not realising that Barry Manilow was in fact singing about the carnival area of Rio de Janeiro named after this Bolivian town.

Copacabana nestled in a bay on the edge of the lake surrounded by two bare rock hills. It was a pretty town, with craft shops and cafés lining the road down to the water, which lapped against a sandy beach. The skyline of warm, orange pantile roofs was dominated by the cathedral, a brilliantly white Moorish-style church with mudéjar domes and blue Portuguese ceramic tiles. The Cerro Calvario, the largest hill that protectively sheltered the town, had the Stations of the Cross dotted along the steep climb to the summit. I thought about walking to the top for the sunset but the religious connotations brought back unwelcome memories of my Catholic childhood, so I settled for watching the sun go down from the water's edge.

∞

The following day I booked myself on a day trip to the Isla del Sol, revered by the Aymara and Quechua people as the birthplace not only of the sun itself but also the two founders of the Inca nation, Manco Capac and Mama Ocllo. The legend says that a long time ago, when the world was full of savages, misery and poverty (not much has changed, then), a brother and a sister, who were also a married couple – Manco Capac and Mama Ocllo – were ordered to leave this island on Lake Titicaca by the sun god and civilise the surrounding peoples. The sun god gave them a golden stick for testing the land for cultivation and eventually the golden stick sank into the ground in the Cuzco Valley, where they began their mission. Manco Capac taught his people how to cultivate and irrigate the land, and to make handicrafts. Mama Ocllo taught the women spinning, weaving and sewing. Thus was born the Inca civilisation.

After a two-hour boat ride, we landed at the south end of the island and were led by our guide up the 206 steps that led to the Fuente del Inca, a natural spring that flows down channels beside the steps. We often had to move aside to allow the locals to pass with their water-carrying donkeys, as there were no vehicles on the island.

It was another hour's walk to the Inca ruins of Pilko Kaina, aptly translated as 'where birds sleep'. Puffing my way up the steep track, I began to think that I'd misread the guidebook, which had indicated that it was a two-kilometre walk across the island; it seemed more than that, but I wondered if that was because every step hurt my legs and my chest so much. After slowly re-inflating my lungs, resting my legs by sitting down for long periods and admiring the almost sheer terracing and views across the lake to the snow-capped Cordillera Real, I was lulled into a false sense of wellbeing and confidently joined the half-dozen youngsters who set off to walk to the north end of the island.

Before long I was struggling to keep up with the energetic youngsters. As my feet began to turn into lumps of concrete, my calves to fill with tangled barbed wire and my lungs to shrink to half their normal size, I just couldn't do it. Like a marathon runner dropped by the leading group, I was powerless to stop the gap growing wider and wider. Feeling wretched, tired and inadequate, I was relieved when a young Swiss girl, also huffing and puffing, dropped back to walk with me.

'I'm tired,' she said. 'After travelling for nine months, I'm no longer impressed by the sights. I think it is time to go home.'

Was that true for me, too? I realised that I'd only half-heartedly admired another set of Inca ruins, and the peaks across the water were only mountains. On reflection, both were worth far more than a cursory inspection. It wasn't only my body that was tired, my mind was too; all the events and sights of the last five-and-a-half months were causing it to overload. Maybe the timing was right to go home. I didn't welcome the thought, as I still wanted to keep going, but walking across the island at this altitude in the strong sun, even at the slow pace we'd now settled for, felt harder than my Nepal trek.

The trail followed the ridge along the centre of the island, mostly just rock and scrub, deserted but for the odd man and donkey. At times both coasts of the island could be seen from the ridge, with the wide lake stretching to the distant mountains. Catching up with the group as they rested at the top of a hill, I learnt that it was in fact twelve kilometres across the island, not two. The Swiss girl and I were the last to struggle into town to catch the boat and, despite the bumpy ride across the lake, I slept all the way back to Copacabana.

Exhausted and with a headache from too much sun, I opted to have my evening meal in the hotel restaurant. The food was fine but the entertainment consisted of a man with a very large drum strapped to his waist and ten panpipe players. They wore white shirts, colourful stripy sashes and bowler hats; the pipers were mostly young boys who should have had L-plates on their back. The band outnumbered the customers and that seemed to inspire them to increase both volume and effort so that my dinner bounced on the table and my head pounded in time with the drumbeats. Several times I'd chided my sons for not emailing more often and I was sorely tempted to buy them each a CD of panpipes, but decided that the punishment was worse than the crime. Gobbling my meal, I fled to my room with my head thumping.

∞

In the morning, as I headed back to Puno and Lima, I was retracing my footsteps for the first time. Until now it had felt as though I had been living in a parallel universe and my previous life bore no relation to the world's ever-moving kaleidoscope. As I looked out of the bus window at Lake Titicaca and sped through villages full of colourful markets and bowler-hatted women, I thought of Ely's Thursday market. How could I bear to exchange beautiful woven fabrics, pottery and jewellery for stalls full of carrots and cauliflowers, outdated William Morris curtain fabric and vacuum cleaner spares (although they did both have potatoes)? How could I swap the Andes for the flat Fens, Machu Picchu for the grassy mound of Cherry Hill, continual motion for my desk at work?

My emotions were as scattered and diverse as the lands I'd visited. While I longed to see my children, I regretted having had so little time in South America. I was becoming resigned to returning home, excited at the prospect of my bed, beer and chocolate – and all that overlaid was with a physical weariness.

With a stopover at Puno before travelling to Juliaca to await yet another flight for Lima, I was aghast when I realised how many presents I had yet to buy. The market traders of Puno had a bumper day as I frantically bought more pots and dishes, squeezing them into the spaces left by the seven long-gone Malaysian toilet rolls.

∞

In Lima, I was to stay with the Torres family, friends of my travelling companion in Malaysia, Mary-Slater. This was the first family that I'd stay with in South America. At the airport Cesar, his wife Lily, and their daughter Miriam appeared waving a sign saying 'Welcome to Peru'. I felt a little embarrassed, not wanting to disappoint them by pointing out that I'd already been in the country for ten days.

Cesar and Lily were short and plump, more Spanish than Indian; their daughters were beautiful dark-haired young girls, into jeans and Western pop. The family was obviously prosperous and lived in an affluent suburb of the city, the house protected by a high electronic fence. Cesar could speak a little English, Lily none, but Miriam was fluent and keen to practise on me.

I'd been overwhelmed by the hospitality I'd received around the world from these tenuous connections, with no questions, no checking me out, just warm welcomes. I don't know why this surprised me as I, too, have taken in wandering foreigners at various times. On finding a young Czech couple sleeping in their car behind my house, I'd given them breakfast and the much-appreciated use of the bathroom. A German lad who knocked on my door was offered a bed for the night but when, uninvited, he'd joined my guests for lunch the next day and settled down for the evening, I decided it was time to ask him to leave. On a business footing, a succession of Italian language students had stayed, one of whom caused great excitement amongst the fen folk as she insisted on hanging her very small smalls in the front window.

Cesar and Lily chauffeured me round the city for the next two days. We visited the large Plaza de Armas, where most of the old buildings had been demolished by earthquakes and replaced by new ones, and the Cathedral with its two yellow towers, which was the oldest building still standing. In one corner was a large bronze statue of Pizarro on horseback; it used to be in the centre of the plaza until the cathedral clergy, sick of their view of the horse's backside, had it moved. The top of the Cerro San Cristóbal, where a seventy-foot cross stands guard over the city, provided magnificent views of the huge sprawling urban mass below. At the Maria Reiche gardens along the seafront, the Nazca Lines have been reproduced and were illuminated at night.

Cesar was keen to know what the outside world thought of Lima. When I confessed that it had a bad reputation for crime, he was a little put out. Minutes later, however, when we were driving through the city, he told me not to leave my bag on the seat beside me but to tuck it underneath out of sight. When we parked to walk to a restaurant, he gave one of the waiting men quite a sum of money to guard the car.

The only problem with these excursions was that I was never told the schedule. When we returned from an outing, everyone disappeared to their rooms for a siesta. Not one for

South America

Plaza de Mayo
Buenos Aires

Bruce and Dancer

Iguazu Falls

Santiago

Atacama Desert

Cusco

Peruvian Fashion

Train to Aquas Calienti

Machu Picchu

Accommodation on Lake Titicaca

Above and below: Tiahuanaco

Above: Road to Corioco
Below: Corioco

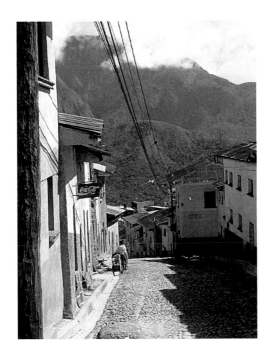

La Paz

Home!

sleeping in the day, I sat in the little garden with Rey the dog until suddenly everyone reappeared, ready to go out again. I had to rush up to my room to change into my one dress, which had more outings in Lima than the previous five months put together.

To me, far more impressive than the sights of Lima were the feasts of Peruvian food and dance to which the Torres family treated me. On the first night in a restaurant in up-market Miraflores, I ate tacu, a black bean mash, while watching the Somos Peru dancers perform a mixture of folk and Spanish-style dances. In one dance, the Alcatraz, the dancers tried to set fire to paper tails hanging from the backs of waistbands. Get that one wrong and it could be very painful.

The following night we went to the Barranco, an artists' and poets' colony, where the jazzy music resembled the Buena Vista Social Club, with guitars and cajón, a wooden box that is sat on and beaten with the fingers. The dancers were from Chincha on the south coast, which has a large black population descended from imported slaves. This was a taste of affluent Lima that I would never have experienced but for the generosity of the Torres family, who wouldn't let me pay for anything however hard I tried. Unlike many other capitals, even the rich areas seemed to have remained very South American; they were not awash with international chains of shops and coffee houses.

It was good to end my South American adventure in such style and in such good company. I had seen another side of city life, albeit the wealthy side, and had stayed with a family rather than wandering alone through the streets. With the Torreses in Lima and Lydia on Amantani Island, I felt I had had a brief but real taste of two very different Peruvian lifestyles.

After Cesar and Lily took me to the airport and waved me off, I found that my ticket had been upgraded, not to business class but to first class, no less. When I asked the steward why, she said that economy was full. Was I just the luckiest person in the world or did Cesar have some hand in this? I will probably never know, as I didn't dare ask him when I emailed my thanks for their hospitality.

Whoever or whatever was responsible, the eleven-hour flight in the lap of luxury ended my South American adventure on a high.

13

The Long Road Home

The excitement of travelling first class temporarily took my mind off the fact that this plane was heading for Europe and home. As I settled down in the spacious high-tech seats, a haughty steward presented me first a glass of sparkling white wine and then with a tan leather bag containing more wash 'n' brush-up equipment than I had brought with me for six months. As he hovered nearby, ready to indulge my every whim (mostly more wine), I was conscious of my scruffy clothes and dusty boots. I tried to act nonchalantly, but my failure to get to grips with the electronic keyboard that worked the first-class gadgets gave me away. Sitting next to me was a taciturn German, his cashmere jumper and immaculately tailored trousers suggesting that he always travelled first class. His face was inscrutable as he showed me how I could raise the leg rest and turn on my personal video monitor. The leg rests were great fun as they go up and down as if in a gym.

Everyone else settled down under a blanket and went to sleep but, despite all the wine, I was wide awake. In about ten hours' time I would be in Spain, then two days later in England. I recalled my long-haul flight to Mumbai (was it really six months ago?), remembering how my mind had shut down rather than consider what lay ahead. I felt very much the same en route to London, preferring to let my mind wander to the places I'd been rather than dwell on what was to come. Unless the plane crashed or I was struck down by an onion-garlanded Barcelona cyclist, I'd have lasted six months without either running, or being stretchered, home.

Mindlessly, I watched a movie and then waggled my legs for a bit, read a book, waggled some more as I listened to music, but it was no good. I couldn't sleep. As Spain grew nearer, I knew that I didn't want to stop there but go straight home. When planning the trip I'd suspected that it would be like this, but a stop in Spain was included in the ticket and, having heard good reports of Barcelona, I'd allotted it a couple of days.

Eventually I drifted off to sleep and in the morning the plane touched down in Madrid, where I transferred to a flight for Barcelona.

∞

Well, here I was back in Europe, the busy Spanish city not looking or sounding very different from a South American city at first. There were no colourful Quechua vendors, the cars were newer, the streets cleaner but, desperately tired and now genuinely homesick, I felt as much a foreigner here as anywhere else in the world.

All I wanted was to find a bed and sleep until I could board the plane home, but that wasn't easy as all the beds in Barcelona seemed to be taken. Exhausted and dispirited, either going up or coming down the various staircases leading to reception desks, I kept passing a young man with a battered suitcase who looked as dejected as me. We started walking together and he told me his name was Karim and he'd just flown in from Algeria. After trudging in and out of the lobbies along the iconic La Rambla, on the point of despair, we found a hotel that had one very expensive double room left.

'We share?' Karim suggested. 'I cannot afford it on my own.'

Hesitating for a moment, I looked hard at Karim.

'It will be OK,' he insisted with a smile.

Having survived for six months, trusting my instincts without mishap, I agreed.

'You share?' asked the hotel receptionist, looking straight

at me with his eyebrows now well above his hairline.

'Yes, we share.'

Both hungry but too tired to walk further than a few metres, we ate a dodgy paella in a far-from-salubrious café. Karim, a waiter, was on his way back to the States, having had to return to Algeria to renew his visa. When he told me he lived in a house with an older woman, for a moment I doubted my trusty instincts.

'What does your partner do?' I asked, hoping she wasn't fifty, in education, with a love of travelling.

'Oh, no, no!' Karim looked aghast. 'I'm only the lodger, she is not my partner.'

Reassured, I relaxed. Exhausted and two days from home, I had neither the desire nor the energy for an Algerian toy boy. There were three single beds in our large room and within minutes we were both sound asleep, with the spare bed safely between us. He was gone by the time I surfaced in the morning, off to catch an early flight to New York.

Thank goodness I'm going home, I thought, or who knows what I'd do next. I chuckled to myself, knowing there was no way I would have allowed a young Arab to share my room six months ago.

∞

After lethargically wandering the city, I sat in a bar with a beer, letting the day drift until it was time for supper. I was getting excited and fidgety, my cleanest and least-faded top was hanging up to de-crease itself for the flight home in the morning, and I was ready to go. It was the last evening of my journey and I opted to eat at a busy pavement restaurant in a brightly lit square, with packed tables shaded by trees thronged by dozens of happy holidaymakers.

I waited for someone to take my order but seemed to have become invisible to the staff. If nothing else, travelling had taught me patience, and I sat quietly watching the scene, contemplating my fellow diners and the end of my journey, while the supercilious waiters careered to and fro bearing trays of tapas and red wine.

The memories of other places and restaurants I had sat in drifted through my mind, along with memories of meals both memorable and memorably awful, from dal bhat to roast guinea pig. By the time I emerged from my reverie I'd been waiting fifteen minutes without a menu. Didn't these waiters know who I was or what evening this was? After an eternity, a stained menu was dropped on my table and I waited another lifetime, unwatered and unfed, until my order was taken seconds before I was about to walk out. My mood changed and I was overwhelmed by a black misery mixed with an irrational anger.

I wanted to scream at the other diners: 'Hey, tourists, this is the last night of my six-month, round-the-world trip! Somebody please talk to me!' None of them looked like Guardian travel supplement readers and they were in family groups, unlikely to want to talk to a lone middle-aged woman with a miserable face. Anyway, I would be home tomorrow, so what was the big deal? But it was a big deal, and I was upset and having difficulty choking back the tears.

Just moments before I gave up the fight and sobbed into my wine, a young American at the next table struck up a conversation. Dennis had the distracted air and enlarged pupils of someone temporarily on another planet, but he could have been Charles Manson for all I cared; he was a knight in shining armour.

'The service is terrible here,' I complained, just as my meal was plonked unceremoniously in front of me. 'Forty-eight hours ago I was eating tacu…' I was off, boring the pants off the poor lad, who smiled benignly and nodded every so often, a faraway look in his flickering eyes.

'Well, it was nice to meet you. Good luck with your studies,' I said as I got up to leave; I had let him talk enough to tell me he was a student. My rage gone, I slept like a baby and the next morning calmly packed the monster bag for the last time and set off for the airport.

∞

Here it was, the end of the adventure. It was difficult to disentangle my emotions as I got on the plane for Heathrow. There was a great sense of achievement at having accomplished my journey, caught every plane, written every Friday report and, if the emails were any indication, entertained the readers – and enjoyed (nearly) every minute. Even flying over the English Channel, I was reluctant to accept that it was over, that there would be no more strange food, exotic dress, dance shows, dodgy planes, trains and buses, lumpy beds and concrete pillows.

At the same time, I couldn't wait to see my children, to have a change of clothes, to dump the monster bag, to sleep in my own bed and to flush the lavatory. Perhaps the biggest dread was of returning to my old life, although in my heart of hearts I knew that there would be little choice but to go back to work. The tiny hope I had of carrying on travelling and writing was all but dead, but even now I wasn't quite ready to deal with this.

The immediate worry was whether anyone would be waiting at the airport, as Ben was in Japan, Rachel at college in Devon and Sam at work. I knew there wouldn't be any brass bands or firework displays from the Guardian, as even a suggestion that I call in at their offices on my way back had been politely deflected.

My excitement mounted as we circled over London and I looked down over the cultivated fields and dense suburbs of Surrey and the M25, as choked as when I left. It was a beautiful sunny day with not a cloud in the sky and England looked fresh and very, very green.

I couldn't get through the formalities quickly enough and danced around impatiently while I waited for my bag. How different it looked from the smart, brand-new bag of six months ago with only one coloured strap remaining (the rest lost to assorted baggage handlers around the world), battered and stained, yet still with two wheels, even if the handle was now bent. It had done well and I let go the hatred I'd felt as I'd had to lug its unwieldy bulk over cobbled streets, stony tracks and up and down narrow hotel staircases.

Proudly, I handed over my precious dog-eared passport and watched the official leaf his way through the pages full of assorted stamps and visas. My heart was thumping as I almost ran to the arrivals area and anxiously looked around. My children hadn't let me down. There was Rachel, Sam and girlfriend waiting with banner, helium balloons and big smiles. It was so lovely to see them, and we hugged and hugged to make up for lost time.

At Sam's flat we paused to drop my bags before heading down to the pub and that long-anticipated pint of IPA. It tasted just as good as I remembered, one sip enough to wipe out the memory of the gassy lager of the last six months. Several pints lined up in front of me, faithful Bruce at my side, the final website photo was taken. After a meal and a lovely night squashed in with Rachel in the spare bed, it was time to take my leave again. Sam had to go to work and Rachel back to Devon for exams.

∞

Alone again, I caught the tube to Kings Cross and the train to Ely. The last train I had been on was to Varanasi in India, a journey that seemed like years ago rather than a mere five months earlier. My mind was full of questions, some of which would be answered when I stepped over my door; others only time would resolve. Would my house be still standing? How bad would the ravages of six months partying be? The lodgers weren't able to move until the weekend, which was a mixed blessing: I didn't return to an empty house but I wouldn't have my own bed for a couple of nights.

Well, Ely Station looked much the same, and there was my house, still standing. I fought my way through the jungle that was once the garden and opened the door with the key that I'd somehow carried around safely for six months. The first thing I noticed was the smell – not the fragrance of young male lodgers but a synthetic odour. I traced it to first one and then six other electric sockets, all garlanded with plug-in air-fresheners. It was disconcerting to see the lodgers' furniture and belongings among my own familiar things, but the cleanliness and orderliness of the house was a surprise. The mountain of bin bags at the back gate gave a clue to the effort it had taken to achieve this, but full marks to the lodgers, Dave and Mark. I was impressed.

Two cats wrapped themselves around my legs and looked at me with accusing eyes, as if to say, 'How could you have left us to such a fate?' Wandering round the house, I touched furniture, my CDs, photos, terminally ill house plants, books and ornaments.

It was hard to believe that the last six months had ever happened, but the lodgers' return from work, the succession of phone calls from friends and a trip to the pub broke the spell.

The next day, Friday, I collected my car and wrote my very last report as a Netjetter. Each press of a key felt like a nail in the coffin of my dreams, forcing me to face the reality that I was home for good. As I wrote, tears dripped onto the keys. It was the end of the adventure.

The weekend passed in a flurry of unpacking, washing, seeing friends and getting photographs developed. The lads moved out on Saturday and I was able to sleep in my lovely bed. When Ben went to Japan in March, he'd left his room as if he'd gone out to post a letter – a cluttered mess, complete with furry mugs and a blanket of dust and grime, but at least it had made me feel close to him as I slept in it until mine was available.

∞

All I wanted to do was relax, rest and reorientate myself, but this was not on the agenda as the dreaded day arrived – Monday – when I had to return to work. Sunday night, I retrieved the case containing my work clothes from the attic, dug out the briefcase, dusted off the work shoes and set the alarm for 6.30am. This was the hardest part of the whole six months; mentally, I just didn't feel ready. Bruce, too, had to go home to Class 6, who had followed his adventures on the internet.

'Well, thank you for your company,' I said, giving him a big hug.

∞

After donning the unfamiliar, now baggy work clothes, forcing my calloused feet into proper shoes and attempting to make my hair presentable, I drove to work. It felt cruel to have to return so quickly, yet it had been my choice to use every day of the six months and not have a respite at the end.

My colleagues were very kind at work that first week, not expecting too much and willing to listen to my many tales. Waiting on my desk were a huge lump of cheese and a big bar of chocolate, both mentioned in one of my reports as objects I'd pined for while away. Everyone commented on how fit and well I looked – as if they had been expecting an emaciated wreck, riddled with exotic digestive disorders and foreign bugs. Despite the tiredness I did feel good, fitter and with less wobbly flesh than for many a year.

Several colleagues had suspected that I might never come back, having been swept off my feet by a maharaja, sheep farmer, yak herder or drug baron. It was embarrassing to confess that there hadn't been a single romantic episode; offers from a lecherous German, a wife-hunting Malaysian, a couple of drunken Balinese and an Argentinian gigolo weren't much to boast about.

After a week at work it was back to normal. There was no time to think as the diary filled up, the fitness faded as car replaced legs, and my lovely forests turned into piles of paper waiting to be read.

It wasn't long before I had to sit down and sort out my finances; the trip had cost me half a year's salary on top of the loss of earnings. With £2,000 of the loan left, the obvious thing to do was to make inroads into my debts but that was far too sensible, so I spent it. First came a new computer with internet, and second a flight to Japan in August to see my eldest son, Ben. It felt good to know I would be travelling again in a couple of months – and anyway, who wants to be rich?

∞

Waiting every day for some response from the Guardian to my return, I tried to be cool and mature but all I felt was hurt and abandoned. After six months of free writing, with not a week missed, I felt that I was due at least a 'welcome home'. After two weeks I could contain myself no longer and sent an email beginning with a mildly caustic 'Is that it, then?' This did provoke a response, with a request for dates to meet up, but after a desultory correspondence when the meeting was put off until after this and after that, I gave up.

By email, I checked in with Sam and Millie, my fellow Netjetters, to find out how they were getting on. Millie was extending her six months and was somewhere in Southeast Asia, glad to be free of the shackles of the weekly report. Sam was, like me, finding both returning and getting any response from the Guardian difficult. I had more luck with Charlie from the travel supplement, who asked for an article on how the Netjetting experience had changed my life. Excited to be writing again, I soon had my fifteen hundred words written and polished, and sent it off. On August 18th, it appeared in the Guardian travel supplement to launch Netjetters 2.

∞

After a month, the longer-term questions were awaiting answers. Could I settle back down and accept my old life back? How much had my life, or had I, really changed? After doing or seeing something new and exciting virtually every day for six months, the return to normality was almost unbearable. I'd forgotten how to cook, television was boring, and I seemed to have lost the ability to concentrate on anything for more than ten minutes.

I was very low. I couldn't let the experience go and the only things stopping me sinking into depression were the thoughts of going to Japan, writing up the trip and playing with my photos on the computer. My mood wouldn't lift and it was only when I gave talks on the trip to local groups that I felt myself come alive again. The first presentation was to my tennis club, where my talk was sandwiched between a sausage dinner and the quiz. The second was to a group of retired Rotarians, who were fascinated by the cost rather than the finer points of backpacking. Finally, there was the local women's group, which involved twenty pensioners gathered in a draughty hall. I considered this a triumph, as one lady came up to me afterwards to congratulate me on being the first speaker she hadn't slept through.

When I got round to reading all the Netjetter stuff in the newspaper and website, I discovered that I had a new identity: the Guardian started every mention of me with 'Sue Stubbings, 51-year-old divorced mother of three.' I was shocked – was that a fair summary of me and my life?

The trip may not have changed my life but I could recognise changes in myself. Travelling on my own, I'd found a strength and confidence that was beyond what I'd expected. To cope with whatever was round the next corner, to interact with new people every day, to survive fear and loneliness, to experience happiness and accept kindness, felt like giant steps on another longer, inner journey towards self-knowledge and self-belief.

I began the redecoration of the house, which developed into an orgy of destruction as the legacy of living out of a bag for six months turned me towards minimalism. All the useless ornaments, surplus furniture, unused gifts, clothes that might come back into fashion if they were kept long enough, shoes that were just too painful to wear, were consigned to the bin or taken to charity shops.

I did, though, cover the walls with photos and the many paintings and hangings that I'd brought back. The thangka Buddhist painting from Kathmandu, miniature artwork from Bali, the Aborigine dot picture with the artist's hair still stuck on the back, the painting of a cabbage tree from New Zealand, the wall hanging from the Uros Islands, all adorned my newly-painted walls.

With the redecoration of my house, I felt that I'd cleansed my old cluttered life as wife, divorcee, mother and student financier, and my house was now a declaration of the new me: Sue Stubbings, independent traveller.